THE GROWTH OF THE LAW

THE GROWTH
OF THE LAW

BY
BENJAMIN N. CARDOZO

GREENWOOD PRESS, PUBLISHERS
WESTPORT, CONNECTICUT

Library of Congress Cataloging in Publication Data

Cardozo, Benjamin Nathan, 1870-1938.
    The growth of the law.

    Reprint of the 1966 ed. published by Yale University
Press, New Haven.
    Includes bibliographical references.
    1. Law--Philosophy. I. Title.
Law   340.1   73-8154
ISBN 0-8371-6953-4

This edition orginally published in 1966 by Yale University
Press, New Haven

Reprinted with the permission of Yale University Press

Reprinted from an original copy in the collections of
Yale University Press

Reprinted by Greenwood Press,
a division of Williamhouse-Regency Inc.

First Greenwood Reprinting 1973
Second Greenwood Reprinting 1975

Library of Congress Catalog Card Number 73-8154

ISBN 0-8371-6953-4

Printed in the United States of America

FOREWORD

CARVED over one entrance to the Yale Law School quadrangle is the sentence: "The Law Is a Living Growth, Not a Changeless Code." Such, in briefest form, is the central message that Judge Cardozo delivered in his second course of lectures at Yale nearly 40 years ago. It was not a wholly new message in 1923; but it was not yet generally accepted by the bench and bar or by the main body of law school instructors. Prior to 1900, no teacher of Cardozo, or of the writer of this Introduction, had presented it to his law students. The subject of study was the "Positive Law," the rules and principles, the true doctrines, the correct definitions. Yet all of these are of human construction, vary with time and circumstance, and constitute merely one large aspect of the evolutionary process of life.

v

Cardozo himself had not held such a theory of law, either as a student or as a practicing lawyer. "I confess that only late in life did a sense of its importance come to me. . . . The problem stood before me in a new light when I had to cope with it as a judge. I found that the creative element was greater than I had fancied." When, only four years before, he had been invited to deliver the Storrs Lectures at Yale, he had replied that he could not accept, because "I have no message to deliver." When it was suggested that he might explain to the law students the process by which he arrived at the decision of a case before him, he at once replied, "I believe I *could* do that." A year's reading and study, in the midst of his judicial labors, told him what his message should be. In four lectures, entitled "The Nature of the Judicial Process,"[1] he presented the part played by the judges as the selective agents of societal evolution, and the intellectual methods by which

---

[1] Benjamin N. Cardozo, *The Nature of the Judicial Process* (New Haven, Yale University Press, 1921).

their choices are made and their results attained. It was indeed a "message" of such vital import and such charm of expression that it hastened his progress from the New York Court of Appeals to the United States Supreme Court.

He was aware that his conception of the judicial process was not the generally accepted one; and he had a slight hesitation about the publication of his lectures. With a touch of humor, he remarked, "If I were to publish them I would be impeached." Not all of the judges of today are conscious of their own judicial process; and on any bench the judge is rare who can make use of it with Cardozo's fineness of perception, his human sympathy and understanding, and his consummate skill of expression. In those lectures he considered the uncertainties of the law, in both its expression and its application, and the "creative" function of the judge.

I was much troubled in spirit, in my first years upon the bench, to find how trackless was the ocean on which I had embarked. I sought for certainty. I was oppressed and disheartened when I found that the quest for it was futile. I was trying to reach land, the solid land of fixed and settled rules, the paradise of a justice that would declare itself by tokens plainer and more commanding than its pale and glimmering reflections in my own vacillating mind and conscience. I found with the voyagers in Browning's "Paracelsus" that the real heaven was always beyond. As the years have gone by, and as I have reflected more and more upon the nature of the judicial process, I have become reconciled to the uncertainty, because I have grown to see it as inevitable. I have grown to see that the process in its highest reaches is not discovery, but creation; and that the doubts and misgivings, the hopes and fears, are part of the travail of mind, the pangs of death and the pangs of birth, in which principles that have served their day expire, and new principles are born.

FOREWORD

Cardozo's second course of lectures, printed in this volume, develop further the course of thought that he had expressed in the earlier course. The two books may be read together with advantage. They show the same erudition, the same keenness of insight, the same charm of expression. Now he is dealing with "the genesis and growth of law, and this involves a study of functions and of ends. What do we mean by law, and how is it created? After it is created, how is it extended or developed?" This is a project more difficult than was the explaining of the judicial process alone. It is not surprising that he is not quite so sure of his ground. But he well knows that human actions and human decisions precede the rules and principles that, at any moment of time, constitute the formal "law." He knows, too, that the rules and principles are human generalizations, inductively based upon the actions, opinions, and decisions; generalizations that, if constructed with industry, insight, and understanding, may be used with advantage as the major premises for new decisions. That is to say, they may be used with advantage until new human thought and experience require a change. They are all tentative working rules, to be respected and used as long as they work to the satisfaction and welfare of men. They are not to be scorned because they are subject to change; they are the only kind of rules we have to guide our steps through life. Injury and death may follow if we disregard them; but injury and death are sure to follow if we treat them as absolutes, without regard to changing numbers and wants and conditions and convictions. It is these that constitute the background and basis that direct human actions and opinions and decisions. It is these, changeable and uncertain and conflicting as they may be, that determine the "Growth of the Law."

Cardozo's discussion of these sources of our decisions and of our rules of law is instructive and intelligent; but it leaves opportunity for much more thought. One who reads Cardozo would profit by a study of William G. Sumner's work on the folkways and mores. These, too, like the "rules of law" that follow them, are changeable with time and circumstance. They, too, are another large aspect of the evolutionary process of life. They constitute a part of the environment into which each one of us is born; the judge and the lawyer as well as the client. As we grow up, we assume their permanence and perfection; and they exercise compelling force over human conduct. It is these that we appeal to in our search for (and in our demands for) "justice," assuming its existence as an "absolute" and the possibility of its human determination and enforcement. This was once often described as "natural justice," as opposed to the human positive law administered by the courts. The compulsive power of the mores over human conduct and the assumption of their permanence have induced many to assert the existence of "natural law," beyond the weak power of man. Cardozo does not adopt these terms; and he knows well that the mores are themselves variable with time and circumstance and tribe, human in origin and development. But it is out of these that rules are formulated and principles asserted; out of these that the "law" has its genesis and growth. Of these sources of law, he says: "They have their roots in the customary forms and methods of business and of fellowship, the prevalent convictions of equity and justice, the complex of belief and practice which we style the *mores* of the day."

On any busy day, there comes before the judge a case for his decision, a case always unique in some degree, greater or less. How shall he decide it, between litigants ardently competing for a favorable decision? Does he have a choice? Is it not foreordained, determined for him with precision by "the law"? First, he consults the "rules and principles," so far as he knows them or can be advised. But rules and principles, although they started at zero in our juristic past, have become so numerous and so variable in form and substance that he cannot know them all; and those that he believes he does know do not convey to him the same thoughts that they convey to other judges. He must make a choice of rules within which to fit his unique case.

Rules and principles are composed of "words"; and words are as slippery as a banana peel. As Holmes has told us, a word is not a "crystal," holding its form and its substance through the ages; it is "the skin of a living thought." But, in itself, a word contains not even the semblance of a thought. It is merely a skin ready to be filled with the thought of its user, to be blown across space until it can spill its contents into the mind of a receiver; and in the spilling there are both losses and accretions. The "meaning" intended by the user may not be identical with that conveyed to the receiver. If this is true of a word, it is doubly true of a rule or principle composed of many words. Even if a rule has been embalmed in the specific words of a written constitution, the men who embalmed them did not fill them with identical thoughts; and through the course of years and events they do not shout identical thoughts to the succeeding generations.

Therefore, the judge must not only make a choice of rules; he must also make a choice of meanings; and in the process he must fit the rule to apply to the unique case before him. In this process, he must always put in something of himself, adding here or subtracting there. A rule is never the same after a new application to a new case. A "rule" is merely a generalization from a number of instances, no two of which were identical; and the content of a rule is no more or less than the sum total of its applications.

In the process of application (that is, in his making a decision), the judge must fit the rule to suit the case; he cannot fit the case to suit the rule. The "case" is made for him, by the parties and the lawyers and (mayhap) by the jury. It is true that instances are not wanting in which a judge has manhandled the case and manipulated the facts, either inadvertently or half consciously. But no clear-minded and intellectually honest judge can do this; he must accept the case that is before him and render a just decision by choosing and fitting the rule to be applied.

A "just decision"! In his unique case! Do not the worded rules and principles constitute "justice" and compel decision? They certainly point toward the goal and narrow the problem. But they are themselves variable and frequently conflicting. In practically all cases, something in addition must influence the decision—the judge's final choice. This addition is found in the folkways and mores of the community of men served by the judge. In Cardozo's words, already quoted above, they are "the customary forms and methods of business and of fellowship, the prevalent convictions of equity and justice, the complex of belief and practice which we style the *mores* of the day." Such is the message of the incomparable judge. It is thus that he divulges both the genesis and the growth of the law.

Cardozo's lectures were prepared for delivery at a law school, to students who already had some experience with legal terms and doctrines and with the decisions and written opinions of the courts. Nonprofessional readers are less well prepared to understand his reasoning and his illustrative cases; but they have already in large numbers found the lectures suggestive and stimulating and have enjoyed the charm of his literary style. To judge the soundness of his conclusions requires the same kind and extent of life experience and reflection that led to his adopting them. But no thoughtful reader can fail to get new insights into the mysteries of human experience, new appreciation of the quality of language, and some awareness that he is in touch with an inspiring personality.

ARTHUR L. CORBIN

New Haven, Connecticut
September 1962

Introductory Note.

THESE lectures, given at the Law School of Yale University in December, 1923 are to be regarded as a supplement to lectures given at the same University in 1921, and published by the Yale University Press under the title of "The Nature of the Judicial Process."

Some thoughts, imperfectly developed in the first series, seemed to call for fuller and more explicit statement in the second, even at some risk of repetition.

B. N. C.

New York, May 30, 1924.

Contents

THE GROWTH OF
THE LAW

I.

Introduction. The Need of a Scientific
Restatement as an Aid to Certainty

THE law of our day faces a twofold need. The first is the need of some restatement that will bring certainty and order out of the wilderness of precedent. This is the task of legal science. The second is the need of a philosophy that will mediate between the conflicting claims of stability and progress, and supply a principle of growth. The first need is deeply felt and widely acknowledged. The American Law Institute, recently organized, is an attempt to meet it. The second, though less generally appreciated, is emerging year by year to fuller recognition.

STABILITY AND PROGRESS

My purpose in these lectures is to say something to you about both, but most of all about the second.

"Law must be stable, and yet it cannot stand still."[1] Here is the great antinomy confronting us at every turn. Rest and motion, unrelieved and unchecked, are equally destructive. The law, like human kind, if life is to continue, must find some path of compromise. Two distinct tendencies, pulling in different directions, must be harnessed together and made to work in unison. All depends on the wisdom with which the joinder is effected.[2] The subject has a literature that takes us back to Aristotle and earlier.[3] Νόμος is to be supplemented by ἐπιείκεια; the tables by the edict; law by equity; custom by statute; rule by discretion. "If we must choose," says Pound in his *Introduction to the Philosophy of Law* (p. 128), "if judicial administration of jus-

[1] Pound, *Interpretations of Legal History*, p. 1.

[2] Vinogradoff, *Common Sense in Law*, p. 122; Coudert, *Certainty and Justice*, p. 1.

[3] Vinogradoff, *Historical Jurisprudence*, vol. II, p. 64; *Common Sense in Law*, p. 209.

tice must of necessity be wholly mechanical or else wholly administrative, it was a sound instinct of lawyers in the maturity of law that led them to prefer the former." Fusion in due proportion is the problem of the ages.

One does not need to expatiate upon the value of certainty in a developed legal system. Law as a guide to conduct is reduced to the level of mere futility if it is unknown and unknowable. Our law stands indicted for uncertainty, and the names of weighty witnesses are endorsed upon the bill. If we seek for causes, there are many. Eight or more were enumerated by the American Law Institute at its organization meeting, adopting the report of a committee. There was the lack of agreement on the fundamental principles of the common law; lack of precision in the use of legal terms; conflicting and badly drawn statutory provisions; attempted distinction between cases where the facts present no distinction in the legal principles applicable; the great volume of recorded decisions; ignorance of judges and lawyers; the number and nature of novel legal

3

questions.[4] Of all these causes, the weightiest, I fancy, is the multiplication of decisions. The fecundity of our case law would make Malthus stand aghast. Adherence to precedent was once a steadying force, the guarantee, as it seemed, of stability and certainty. We would not sacrifice any of the brood, and now the spawning progeny, forgetful of our mercy, are rending those who spared them.[5] Increase of numbers has not made

[4] It is interesting to match this catalogue of grievances against the catalogue made by Bacon in his proposal for amending the laws of England, some three hundred years ago (Bacon, *Law Tracts*, p. 5). "Certain it is, that our laws, as they now stand, are subject to great incertainties, and variety of opinion, delays and evasions; whereof ensueth, (1) That the multiplicity and length of suits is great; (2) That the contentious person, is armed, and the honest subject wearied and oppressed; (3) that the judge is more absolute; who, in doubtful cases, hath a greater stroke and liberty; (4) that the chancery courts are more filled, the remedy of law being often obscure and doubtful; (5) that the ignorant lawyer shroudeth his ignorance of law, in that, doubts are frequent and many; (6) That men's assurances of their lands and estates by patents, deeds, wills, are often subject to question, and hollow; and many the like inconveniences."

[5] Stone, "Some Aspects of the Problem of Law Simplification," 23 *Columbia Law Review* 319; Salmond, "The Literature of Law," 22 *Columbia Law Review* 197, 199.

for increase of respect. The output of a multitude of minds must be expected to contain its proportion of vagaries. So vast a brood includes the defective and the helpless. An avalanche of decisions by tribunals great and small is producing a situation where citation of precedent is tending to count for less, and appeal to an informing principle is tending to count for more. Crowded dockets make it impossible for judges, however able, to probe every case to its foundations. Even if time were adequate, the case, as it comes before a court, is specific, concrete, the general shrouded in particulars. With the mind directed to these particulars, inevitably it will happen, in view of the limitations of human vision, that the universal element will sometimes be lost sight of in its wrappings, the larger truth ignored, though it fills the background of the landscape, because our eyes are fixed upon the smaller one that lies before us at our feet. This danger, great as it has always been, grows greater every day as mass and maze increase. The very strength of our common law, its cautious advance

5

and retreat a few steps at a time[6] is turned into a weakness unless bearings are taken at frequent intervals, so that we may know the relation of the step to the movement as a whole. One line is run here; another there. We have a filigree of threads and cross-threads, radiating from the center, and dividing one another into sections and cross-sections. We shall be caught in the tentacles of the web, unless some superintending mind imparts the secret of the structure, lifting us to a height where the unity of the circle will be visible as it lies below. The perplexity of the judge becomes the scholar's opportunity.

A movement justifying the hope that the opportunity will not be lost is already under way. The American Law Institute, organized at Washington in February, 1923, is the first coöperative endeavor by all the groups engaged in the development of law to grapple with the monster of uncertainty and slay him. It proposes a scientific and accurate restatement of the law in specially

[6] Pound, "Courts and Legislation," 7 *Am. Pol. Science Rev.* 361; IX Modern Legal Philosophy Series, p. 214.

selected fields. The fields that have been marked for entry at the outset are contracts, torts, conflict of laws, and agency. Others will be chosen later. The restatement will consist, first, of a summary of principles stated with such fullness as will afford an adequate presentation of the subject, somewhat after the manner of Dicey's *Conflict of Laws* or Stephen's *Digest of the Law of Evidence;* and, second, of such amplification, illustration, and explanation as shall be necessary to the complete understanding and practical application of the principles, the same works that I have mentioned again supplying an approximate example. Accompanying each restatement there will be a treatise which is to consist of a complete exposition of the present condition of the law and a full citation of authorities. It is to analyze and discuss all the legal problems presented, and justify the statement of the law set forth in the principles. Professor Williston of Harvard will draft the statement of the law of contracts, and the treatise to go with it. Among the critics of his work will be Professor Corbin of Yale, Professor Page of Wisconsin, and Professor Oliphant of Columbia. Professor Bohlen of the University of Pennsylvania, assisted by Professor Young B. Smith of Columbia, Dean Hepburn of Indiana, Professor Goodrich of Michigan, and Professor Thurston of Yale will state the law of torts. Professor Beale of Harvard will deal with the conflict of laws after first reconciling his own conflicts with Professor Lorenzen of Yale, Professor Bigelow of Chicago, Professor Buchanan of Pittsburgh, and Professor Goodrich of Michigan. Professor Mechem of the University of Chicago will state the law of agency. The groups of critics and advisers are not constant, but from time to time, as occasion prompts, are varied or enlarged. The statement of the draftsman, tentative and provisional in its beginnings, will be subject to suggestion and revision at the hands of his associates, leaders, all, of juristic thought. It will then be submitted to the Council and the members of the Institute. After emerging from their scrutiny, it will be either accepted as adequate or referred back to

8

its authors. When, finally, it goes out under the name and with the sanction of the Institute, after all this testing and retesting, it will be something less than a code and something more than a treatise. It will be invested with unique authority, not to command, but to persuade. It will embody a composite thought and speak a composite voice. Universities and bench and bar will have had a part in its creation.

I have great faith in the power of such a restatement to unify our law. Of course, like anything else worthy of success, it must justify itself by the way in which it is done. Unless it is done with superlative skill, it will fail and ought to fail. None the less, the plan reduces to a minimum the likelihood of failure. If these men cannot restate the law, then the law is incapable of being restated by anyone. You must not think of the product as a code, invested with the binding force of statute. The only force it will possess, at least at the beginning, will be its inherent power of persuasion. Restatement is needed, "not to repress the forces through which judge-made law develops, but to stimulate and free them."[7] "The judicial process is to be set in motion again, but with a new point of departure, a new impetus and direction. In breaking one set of shackles, we are not to substitute another. We are to set the judges free."[8] No doubt there will be a strong presumption in favor of the principle or the precept that can vouch such sponsors to its aid. The thought was happily stated by Mr. Root at the organization of the Institute in his address as chairman of the meeting: "Any lawyer, whose interest in litigation requires him to say that a different view of the law shall be taken, will have upon his shoulders the burden to overturn the statement. Instead of going back through ten thousand cases, it will have been done for him; there will not be a conclusive presumption, but a practical *prima facie* statement upon which, unless it is overturned, judgment may rest." We know how much can be done by one man, acting and speaking only

[7] 35 *Harv. L. R.* 113, 117.
[8] 35 *Harv. L. R., supra.*

for himself, to build up a common law. Kent and Story did it in their day. Williston and Wigmore are doing it in ours. One dare not estimate the number of sane and sound judgments, useful members of society, that would have been brought into the world defective and deformed without the guidance of these masters. They have shown what can be done for law by a wise science of eugenics. If all this can be accomplished by individual initiative and endeavor, how much greater will be the authority of one who speaks, not merely in his own name, but in that of an organized profession.

More and more we are looking to the scholar in his study, to the jurist rather than to the judge or lawyer, for inspiration and for guidance. Historians tell us that in olden days the practice was much followed by the German courts "of sending up the documents of a case to the law faculty of a university of some standing—Halle, Greifswald, Jena—in order to obtain a consultation as to the proper decision."[9] A tendency dif-

[9] Vinogradoff, *Common Sense in Law,* p. 203;

ferent from this, and yet recalling it in many ways, can be traced even now in the progress of our law. Extra-judicial agencies are assuming an importance that increases year by year. Chief of these agencies is the criticism and the suggestion of scholars in the universities and in other institutes of learning. Until the rise of the modern law school with its critical method, there was no organ through which professional opinion could disclose itself effectively and promptly. The bar was, indeed, there, but its reaction was slow and casual. It was too loosely organized and too busy at times about winning its own cases to be vigilant, in season and out, for the symmetry of legal science. Sometimes, it is true, when a court had gone woefully astray, there would develop in the course of years an undercurrent of hostile judgment which at intervals

Stammler, "Modern Jurisprudence," 21 *Michigan Law Rev.* 877, 878; *cf.* the *Responsa Prudentium of Roman Law;* Muirhead, *Roman Law,* pp. 291-293; J. M. Gest, "Notes upon Legal Continental Literature," 69 *Univ. of Pennsylvania Law Rev.* 128, 129; Hadley, *Rome and the World Today* 238, 242, recalling Shakespeare's "Merchant of Venice."

would well up and emerge above the surface. The same thing might happen, and more promptly, if the case was a conspicuous one, exciting public interest. Criticism, however, was in the main sporadic and unorganized, and limited too often to muttered disapproval, hardly vocal or audible, and only slowly, if at all, communicated to those whose work was disapproved. The universities have given us for the first time a body of critics ever on the watch.

This new organ of expression is the university law review. I have spoken of the works of Williston and Wigmore which took the rank of classics almost overnight. Hardly less notable are the studies in smaller fields which are made month by month in the columns of the reviews. In the preface to one of the supplements of his treatise on Evidence, Wigmore complains, writing in 1915, that the courts were unwilling, as it seemed, to refer to the masters of juristic thought unless the products of their labor were published in a volume. Anything *bound* might be cited, though wrought through no process more intel-

lectual than the use of paste pot and scissors.
Pamphlets were anathema. It is perhaps signifi-
cant that in the preface to the last edition he
omits the caustic comment. Judges have at last
awakened, or at all events a number of them
not wholly negligible, to the treasures buried in
the law reviews. A recent case in New York will
illustrate my meaning, and show the power of
the universities to guide the course of judgment.
We had a series of decisions dealing with a supposed rule that in actions for specific perform-
ance there must be mutuality of remedy, and
mutuality, not merely at the time of the decree,
but at the making of the contract. Some cases,
repeating the words of Fry and Pomeroy, went
pretty far in exalting the supposed rule into one
of general application. I have little doubt that
if the university professors had not intervened,
the rule would have been extended by a process
of purely logical deduction, and things would
have gone from bad to worse. In the meantime
the professors in the universities became busy,
and pointed out where we were tending. Ames

started the crusade in an early number of the *Columbia Law Review*.[10] Lewis of Pennsylvania strengthened the attack, advancing from a somewhat different angle, in a series of papers in the *American Law Register*.[11] More recently Dean Stone of Columbia, writing in the *Columbia Law Review*,[12] exposed the dangers of the course that many of the courts were following. Finally Professor Williston summarized the arguments and the precedents in his treasury of learning.[13] Only the other day, the Court of Appeals reconsidered the whole subject, and put it on a basis which will be found consistent, so, at least, I hope, with equity and justice.[14] But the interesting thing about the episode is the part that was played by extra-judicial agencies. Without the critical labors of Ames and Lewis and Stone and Williston, the heresy, instead of dying out, would

[10] 3 *Col. L. R.* 1; *Lectures on Legal History,* p. 370.
[11] 40 *Am. Law Register,* N.S., 270, 382, 447, 507, 559; 42 *id.* 591.
[12] 16 *Col. L. R.* 443.
[13] 3 Williston, *Contracts,* secs. 1433, 1436, 1440.
[14] Epstein v. Gluckin, 233 N. Y. 490.

probably have persisted, and even spread. It would have gained new vitality with every judgment that confirmed it. Inevitably, too, the process of logic or of development by analogy would have pushed it forward into new fields. What saved the day was criticism from without.

I have little doubt, therefore, that the proposed restatement will prove a potent force in bringing certainty and order out of our wilderness of precedent. "He who has not a copy of Azo's books," ran the proverb of the Middle Ages, "need not go to the Courts of Justice."[15] So men will come in time to speak of the publications of the Institute. We shall turn to their pages before turning anywhere else. Often we shall go no farther. They will accumulate with the years a power and prestige that will level opposition. Little by little the courts, even though nonconformist at the beginning, will tend to conformity and unity. Two words of caution, however, we must keep with us. In our worship of certainty, we must distinguish between the

[15] Vinogradoff, *Common Sense in Law*, p. 202.

sound certainty and the sham, between what is gold and what is tinsel; and then, when certainty is attained, we must remember that it is not the only good; that we can buy it at too high a price; that there is danger in perpetual quiescence as well as in perpetual motion; and that a compromise must be found in a principle of growth.

I have said that there is a certainty that is genuine and a certainty that is illusory, a symmetry that is worth attaining and a symmetry to be shunned. One of the reasons why our law needs to be restated is that judges strive at times after the certainty that is sham instead of the certainty that is genuine. They strive after a certainty that will keep the law consistent within their own parish, their little territorial jurisdictions, instead of the certainty that will keep it consistent with verities and principles as broad as the common law itself, and as deep and fundamental as the postulates of justice. The tendency is insidious and to some extent inevitable. Particular precedents are carried to conclusions which are thought to be their logical development. The end is not foreseen. Every new decision brings the judge a little farther. Before long he finds himself in a dilemma. He does not like the spot where he is placed, yet he is unwilling and perhaps unable to retreat from it. The certainty that is arrived at by adherence to precedent is attained, but there is a sacrifice of another certainty that is larger and more vital. This latter certainty is lost if we view the law in shreds and patches, not steadily and whole with a sweep that reaches the horizon. Often a spurious consistency is preserved by artificial and unreal distinctions. The idol is discredited, but he is honored with lip service, the rubrics of the ancient ritual. We must have the courage to unmask pretense if we are to reach a peace that will abide beyond the fleeting hour. The law's uncertainties are to be corrected, but so also are its deformities. Often they go together, and the remedy that cures the one will be found to cure the other. Restatement must include revision when the vestiges of organs, atrophied by disuse, will become centers of infection if left within the social body.

My second caution, however, is the weightier. Overemphasis of certainty may carry us to the worship of an intolerable rigidity. If we were to state the law today as well as human minds can state it, new problems, arising almost overnight, would encumber the ground again. "As in other sciences, so in politics, it is impossible that all things should be precisely set down in writing; for enactments must be universal, but actions are concerned with particulars."[16] Restatement will clear the ground of débris. It will enable us to reckon our gains and losses, strike a balance, and start afresh. This is an important, an almost inestimably important, service. But hereafter, as before, the changing combinations of events will beat upon the walls of ancient categories. "Life has relations not capable of division into inflexible compartments. The moulds expand and shrink."[17] Existing rules and principles can give

[16] Aristotle, *Politics,* Book II, Jowett's translation.
[17] Glanzer v. Shepard, 233 N. Y. 236, 241.

us our present location, our bearings, our lati-
tude and longitude. The inn that shelters for
the night is not the journey's end. The law, like
the traveler, must be ready for the morrow. It
must have a principle of growth.

II.

The Need of a Philosophy of Law as an Aid to Growth. The Problems of Legal Philosophy. The Meaning and Genesis of Law

I AM brought thus to the second phase of my discourse, the need of a philosophy of law. The theorist has a hard time to make his way in an ungrateful world. He is supposed to be indifferent to realities; yet his life is spent in the exposure of realities which, till illumined by his searchlight, were hidden and unknown. He is contrasted, and to his great disfavor, with the strenuous man of action, who ploughs or builds or navigates or trades, yet, in moments of meditation he takes the consoling knowledge to his heart that the action of his favored brothers would be futile unless informed and inspired by thoughts that came from him. Of the lot of all theorists, that of the philosopher is the sorriest. He is the theorist κατ' ἐξοχήν. Let us heave a stone at him, say his enemies, and thus stigmatize his tribe. "I thought the man had sense," said the Duchess of Marlborough when she quarreled with Voltaire; "but I find him at bottom either a fool or a philosopher."[1] General truths are hard to grasp. Most of us have all we can do in accumulating by dint of toil the knowledge of a few particulars. A troublesome lot, these men who are searching always for the ultimate. If we cannot understand, let us show that the superiority is ours by combining to deride.

I have made myself today the self-appointed spokesman and defender of the philosopher in the field of law. I am not concerned to vindicate philosophy, either in jurisprudence or outside of it, as an inquiry of cultural value or speculative interest. Pretensions, thus limited, would perhaps be feebly contested, or even grudgingly allowed. My concern is with the relation of phi-

[1] Quoted by Strachey, *Books and Characters*, p. 125.

losophy to life. The significance of this relation should be brought home to the student while he is yet standing on the threshold. You think perhaps of philosophy as dwelling in the clouds. I hope you may see that she is able to descend to earth. You think that in stopping to pay court to her, when you should be hastening forward on your journey, you are loitering in bypaths and wasting precious hours. I hope you may share my faith that you are on the highway to the goal. Here you will find the key for the unlocking of bolts and combinations that shall never be pried open by clumsier or grosser tools. You think there is nothing practical in a theory that is concerned with ultimate conceptions. That is true perhaps while you are doing the journeyman's work of your profession. You may find in the end, when you pass to higher problems, that instead of its being true that the study of the ultimate is profitless, there is little that is profitable in the study of anything else.[2]

[2] *Cf.* Tourtoulon, *Philosophy in the Development of Law,* vol. XIII, Modern Legal Philosophy Series, Professor Cohen's Introduction, p. 24.

THE PROBLEMS OF PHILOSOPHY

At the outset, let us try to get some notion of what a philosophy of law includes. There is no need to mark its content by unvarying or rigid lines. It is enough to indicate some things that are certain to fall within its limits. We shall thus evade difficulties of definition which a philosophy of law shares with philosophy in general. "The moment you attempt to define its subject matter," says Windelband in his recent *Introduction to Philosophy*,[3] "you find the philosophers themselves failing you. There is no such thing as a generally received definition of philosophy, and it would be useless to reproduce the innumerable attempts that have been made to provide one."[4] Description may serve where definition would be hazardous. A philosophy of law will tell us how law comes into being, how it grows, and whither it tends. Genesis and development and end or function, these things, if no others, will be dealt with in its pages. To

[3] *Introduction to Philosophy*, by Wm. Windelband, translated by Joseph McCabe, p. 20.
[4] *Cf.* Wm. James, *Some Problems of Philosophy*, p. 29; Royce *The Spirit of Modern Philosophy*, p. 1.

these it will probably add a description of the genesis and growth and function, not only of law itself, but also of some of those conceptions that are fundamental in the legal framework. One who wishes to get a notion of the contour of the field can do no better than consult the brilliant *Introduction to a Philosophy of Law* by the Dean of the Harvard Law School. One will find there little of merely abstract definition, of diagrams and maps and charts. One will see the fields as they are tilled, and gain a sense of their value by tasting of their fruits.

The genesis, the growth, the function, and the end of law—the terms seem general and abstract, too far dissevered from realities, raised too high above the ground, to interest the legal wayfarer. But believe me, it is not so. It is these generalities and abstractions that give direction to legal thinking, that sway the minds of judges, that determine, when the balance wavers, the outcome of the doubtful lawsuit. Implicit in every decision where the question is, so to speak, at large, is a philosophy of the origin and aim of law, a philosophy which, however veiled, is in truth the final arbiter. It accepts one set of arguments, modifies another, rejects a third, standing ever in reserve as a court of ultimate appeal. Often the philosophy is ill coördinated and fragmentary. Its empire is not always suspected even by its subjects. Neither lawyer nor judge, pressing forward along one line or retreating along another, is conscious at all times that it is philosophy which is impelling him to the front or driving him to the rear. None the less, the goad is there. If we cannot escape the Furies, we shall do well to understand them.

My approach to the subject will be by asking you to consider at the outset the nature of the judicial process. The lawyer cannot rise to the full measure of his power in persuading, nor the judge to the full measure of *his* power in deciding, without an understanding of the process which the one attempts to control and the other to pursue. Analysis of the judicial process involves analysis of the genesis and growth of law, and this involves a study of functions and of ends. What do we mean by law, and how is it created? After it is created, how is it extended or developed? What are the principles that guide the choice of paths when the judge, without controlling precedent, finds himself standing uncertain at the parting of the ways? What are the directive forces to be obeyed, the methods to be applied, the ends to be sought? These are problems of philosophy. Every decision, where the judicial process is creative, and not merely static or declaratory, is a reflection of the problem and an expression of the answer. The philosophy may be inconsistent or unsound or distorted. The answers will share the vice, and be perverse or unwise or contradictory. The problem is always present. We shall not find the solution by acting as if there were nothing to be solved.

Let me first consider what we are to understand by "law," at least for the purpose of the inquiry on which we are embarking. We must know what law is, or at any rate what we mean by it, before we can know how it develops. Isolate or try to isolate this little patch upon the web of human thought, and you will be given some hint of the unifying threads that are shot through the fabric of our knowledge. Queries that were propounded in the beginnings of recorded thought turn up in unexpected regions, and press us for an answer. Philosophy has her feuds that heed no truce of God. For several thousand years she has been trying to compose them, yet it is only with indifferent success that she has kept the peace within her borders. The tyro in legal studies may thus be pardoned some surprise and petulance when he finds the borders trenching upon the precincts of the law. Here at least, he has said to himself, here at least is a quiet nook where my ears will not be assailed with the babble of contending schools. The chatter of nominalist and realist, waging their never ending war of words, will not penetrate these sheltered fields. Platonist and Aristotelian will here know themselves as brothers. Vain is his thought. The promised haven is not found. At the very threshold of his study, when he seeks a definition of law itself, the ancient factions are before him, already at each other's throats. Is there any law beyond the precept of isolated judgments? Must we surrender the quest for the universal, and content ourselves with what is merely a succession of particulars? Back of the changing phenomena are we to posit a substratum which gives coherence and reality? These are not questions suggested by the study of mediaeval schoolmen. They were not propounded by Aquinas. The student will have to grapple with them if he would understand his Blackstone. Every now and then he will be reminded of their bearing upon present-day realities. He tries to console himself with the thought that peace awaits him later. All this, he argues, is but preliminary. When I am fairly launched upon my subject, I shall gain the open sea. He opens a book on corporations, and seeks to understand the nature of juristic persons. Nominalist and realist are at each other's throats again. One of the factions has it that the corporation is but a name or symbol for an aggregate of men and women. The other faction tells him that beyond the name and the components there is in very truth a *tertium quid*. Some of the bitterest controversies of the law preserve the ancient feud today.[5] Platonist and Aristotelian flock to the standards of their leaders. The air resounds again with the slogans of the schools.

Our concern for the moment is with conflicting theories of the nature of law itself. With all the bitterness of the conflict, it is in part a war of words. A good deal of the warfare has its origin in the confusion that arises when a single term of broad and ill-defined content is made to do duty without discrimination for two or more

[5] Saleilles, *De la personnalité juridique;* Vinogradoff, *Common Sense in Law,* p. 77; Barker, *Political Thought from Spencer to Today,* p. 175; Maitland, Introduction to Gierke's *Political Theories of the Middle Age,* XVIII; Maitland, *Coll. Papers,* 3, pp. 304, 314; Buckland, *Roman Law,* pp. 175, 176; Henderson, *The Position of Foreign Corporations in American Constitutional Law,* p. 3. "The problem of the one and the many lies at the bottom of all logic, of all ethics, of all economics, and of all politics," Nicholas Murray Butler, address at the Hague on "The Development of the International Mind," July 20, 1923, vol. IX, *Am. Bar Assn. Jour.,* p. 520.

ideas. Dean Pound in a recent essay[6] bewails "the ambiguity of the term 'law' that requires us to use one word for the legal precepts which are actually recognized and applied in the tribunals of a given time and place, and for the more general body of doctrine and tradition from which those precepts are chiefly drawn, and by which we criticize them." The attempt of some jurists to confine law in its proper sense to the first of these meanings, involving a refusal to extend it to the second, ends in a sceptical nihilism which is the negation of all law. What is left is not a body of rules of general application, but mere isolated judgments, binding upon the parties only, and losing their quality of law in the very moment that they gain it. I have had occasion elsewhere to develop this point more fully.[7] I have shown, too, how varying views of the nature and origin of law may lead to varying decisions upon the merits of a lawsuit. What are

[6] Judge Holmes's "Contributions to the Science of Law," 34 *Harv. L. R.* 449, 452.

[7] *Nature of the Judicial Process*, p. 126.

31

the rights of litigants who have acted upon a judgment of the highest court of a state to the effect that a statute is invalid, if a controversy between them comes before the same court after the earlier judgment has been overruled? You will find it hard to reach a solution of such a problem without wandering into a philosophical dissertation upon the nature of law in general. Some difficulties and ambiguities that beset the jurists of continental Europe have, indeed, been spared us. We do not need to spend pages in an attempted demonstration that *Gesetz* is not co-terminous with *Recht*,[8] that *la loi* is narrower than *le droit*,[9] that law is something more than statute. We are saved from all this because in action every day about us is the process by which forms of conduct are stamped in the judicial mint as law, and thereafter circulate freely as part of the coinage of the realm. But even before that stage is reached, there has not been lacking altogether the element of coercive power.

[8] Ehrlich, *Grundlegung der Soziologie des Rechts.*
[9] Duguit, *Traité de droit constitutionnel.*

Men go about their business, and regulate their affairs with serenity and safety, though the principle or rule or standard to which they adhere for guidance or enlightenment is without the sanction of a judgment, and even more frequently without the sanction of a statute. At some point back of definitive adjudication, of perfect or unfailing certainty, we reach the stage of law.

If you ask what degree of assurance must attach to a principle or a rule or a standard not yet embodied in a judgment before the name of law may properly be affixed to it, I can only fall back upon a thought which I shall have occasion to develop farther, the thought that law, like other branches of social science, must be satisfied to test the validity of its conclusions by the logic of probabilities rather than the logic of certainty. When there is such a degree of probability as to lead to a reasonable assurance that a given conclusion ought to be and will be embodied in a judgment, we speak of the conclusion as law, though the judgment has not yet been rendered, and though, conceivably, when rendered, it may disappoint our expectation. I think it is interesting to reflect that such a use of the term law strengthens the analogy between the law which is the concern of jurisprudence, and those principles of order, the natural or moral laws, which are the concern of natural or moral science. The pendulum has swung back and forth a good many times, but the tendency of juristic thought today involves emphasis upon the elements of agreement rather than the elements of difference.[10]

It was not always so. In the days, now too remote, of my study in a law school, authors and teachers delighted to dwell on the antithesis between law that was truly law, and law masquerading in borrowed plumes, with no better claim of title than metaphor or remote analogy. Law that was truly law was to be the subject of our study. We were not to look for it anywhere except in statute or decision, and hardly perhaps in statute. Its personification was the sheriff, and

[10] *Cf.* Charmont, *Renaissance du droit naturel.*

34

the test of its reality a writ. Law by metaphor or analogy was merely a principle of order. We might recognize the kinship if we chose, but always in the spirit of condescension that is due to poor relations. It would do no harm to humor the planets, or gratify their sense of pride, by saying it was law that governed their majestic movements. All the time, however, we should remember that the poor relations must know their place, and keep within the bounds of moderation the claims of distant kinship. Tide and eclipse and the changing seasons of the year display, we were told, a uniformity of their own. We were not to confuse it with the sequence revealed to faithful eyes after long and patient scrutiny in the judgments of the courts. The uniformities of the equinoxes might be deeper and more obvious than those of the decisions construing the statute of frauds in its fourth and seventeenth sections. None the less, coherence, if lacking in the commentary, was balanced and compensated by the presence of something else. The product of judicial exegesis might seethe and teem with incongruities. We were consoled at least by the assurance that it had something more important. It had the quality of law.

The passing years have not brought to me the gift of wisdom, but they have at least opened my eyes to the perception that distinctions which in those early days seemed sharp and obvious are in truth shadowy and blurred, the walls of the compartments in no wise water-tight or rigid. In particular, I see that the relationship is closer than I fancied between the principles of order which, to my early thinking, were laws by brevet or courtesy, and the Simon-pure creations of state power, functioning in all the plenitude of sovereignty through its appointed agencies, the courts. If once I figured the two families as distant kinsmen, tracing their lines perhaps to a common ancestor, but so remotely and obscurely that the call of blood might be ignored, I have now arrived at the belief that they are cousins german, if not brothers.

Law is something more than a succession of isolated judgments which spend their force as law when they have composed the controversies that led to them. "The general body of doctrine and tradition" from which the judgments were derived, and "by which we criticize them"[11] must be ranked as law also, not merely because it is the chief subject of our study, but because also the limits which it imposes upon a judge's liberty of choice are not purely advisory, but involve in greater or less degree an element of coercive power. At all events, if this is not law, some other word must be invented to describe it; and to it we shall then transfer the major portion of our interest. Judgments themselves have importance for the student so far, and so far only, as they permit a reasonable prediction that like judgments will be rendered if like situations are repeated. The study of the law is thus seen to be the study of principles of order revealing themselves in uniformities of antecedents and consequents. When the uniformities are sufficiently constant to be the subject of prediction

[11] Pound, *supra*.

with reasonable certainty, we say that law exists. Indeed, they may be so persuasive and compelling as to lead us to say, if the prediction miscarries, that the judgment which disappoints us is error, or false law—at all events, if we have the hardihood to disregard the warning of Holland and others that false law is a misnomer, and that law, like grammar, is superlative. We may even hazard a new prediction that the judgment which gives momentary currency to error will some day be reversed. On the other hand, situations may exist where the uniformities are so inconstant, the analogies so doubtful, the body of principles and tradition so equivocal in their directions, that we are unable to predict. We can at most argue or suggest. No doubt there is difficulty, upon occasion, in fixing the point of time at which one process shades into the other. When does a mere hypothesis become transformed into a principle or a rule, and when does the principle or rule put off the vestments of authority, and become a shattered or deposed hypothesis? Falling back upon my logic of probabilities, I can do no better than point my meaning by the aid of concrete illustrations.

We speak of it as a rule of law today that mutual promises give rise to a contract, and their breach to a right of action for damages. We know this was not always so.[12] We can name the case whereby the rule as we know it was established.[13] Until the judgment in Strangborough v. Warner, 4 Leon 3, decided in 1588, there had been in English law the most fragmentary and imperfect development of contract by mere consent. Before the rendition of that judgment, we cannot say with justice that there was a preëxisting principle or rule which the judges were extending or applying. They formulated the principle or rule themselves, and gave it potency thereafter by a process of creation. Suppose some court today should refuse to accept the judgment in Strangborough's case,

[12] Holdsworth, *History of English Law*, vol. II, p. 72; Ames, *History of Parol Contracts Prior to Assumpsit*, III Anglo-Am. Legal Essays 304.
[13] Sweet, *Foundations of Legal Liability*, vol. II, p. 55.

and hold the contract void. The ruling might involve an abuse of power, or flagrant error, but the judgment, unless reversed upon appeal, would, none the less, be binding upon the parties, and express the law for them. With this possibility before us, with the power residing in the court to nullify all our predictions, why do we, none the less, declare with assurance that this case is still to be accepted as a statement of the law? We do so because the observation of recorded instances almost without number induces a belief which has the certainty of conviction that the rule will be acted on as law by the agencies of government. As in the processes of nature, we give the name of law to uniformity of succession.[14]

Let me pass now to an illustration where the answer is more doubtful. A maker of automobiles is sued by the victim of an accident. The plaintiff bought the vehicle, not from the maker, but from someone else. He asserts that there was

[14] *Cf.* Vinogradoff, *Common Sense in Law,* pp. 206, 207.

40

negligence in the process of manufacture, and that privity of contract is unnecessary to confer a right of action. Since the decision in Mac-Pherson v. Buick Mfg. Co., 217 N. Y. 382, decided in 1916, the law of New York must be said to be in accordance with the plaintiff's claim. What, however, was the posture of affairs before the Buick case had been determined? Was there any law on the subject? A mass of judgments, more or less relevant, had been rendered by the same and other courts. A body of particulars existed on which an hypothesis might be reared. None the less, their implications were equivocal. We see this in the fact that the judgment of the court was not rendered without dissent. Whether the law can be said to have existed in advance of the decision, will depend upon the varying estimates of the nexus between the conclusion and existing principle and precedent.

Let me take another case where the problem was yet more doubtful. Suppose a decision frankly new, covering a virgin field,[15] or a deci-

[15] Hynes v. N. Y. Central R. R. Co., 231 N. Y. 229.

sion reached as the result of the upsetting of another judgment.[16] Klein v. Maravelas held valid the sales in bulk act, and in so doing overruled an earlier decision which held it void. People v. Schweinler Press held valid the statute limiting hours of work for women, overruling an earlier decision to the contrary. Epstein v. Gluckin qualified the scope of earlier decisions which had made mutuality of remedy a condition of equitable relief, and did this in recognition of extra-judicial criticism of the earlier and narrower view. In all these qualifying or overruling judgments, appeal was made to a body either of judicial or of professional opinion which displayed uniformities at variance with the judgment to be nullified or limited. A wrong answer was set right by the substitution of the true one. The quality of law was maintained as the expression through the courts of a principle of order.

Now, we must note that in all these cases

[16] Klein v. Maravelas, 219 N. Y. 383; People v. Schweinler Press, 214 N. Y. 395; cf. Epstein v. Gluckin, 233 N. Y. 490.

there was present the possibility that the prediction would miscarry. The distinction in that respect between one case and another is one merely of degree. So, indeed, it must always be. The court may reverse itself, and unsettle what seemed settled. It may ignore or misapply established rules through carelessness or ignorance or in rare instances corruption. What permits us to say that the principles are law is the force or persuasiveness of the prediction that they will or ought to be applied. Even when the conclusion upon a special state of facts is in doubt, as in the case of the manufacturer of the Buick car, there is little doubt that the conclusion will be drawn from a stock of principles and rules which will be treated as invested with legal obligation. The court will not roam at large, and light upon one conclusion or another as the result of favor or caprice. This stock of rules and principles is what for most purposes we mean by law We may not draw the same deductions from them as the court does in this case or in that There will be little difference in our premises.

We shall unite in viewing as law that body of principle and dogma which with a reasonable measure of probability may be predicted as the basis for judgment in pending or in future controversies. When the prediction reaches a high degree of certainty or assurance, we speak of the law as settled, though, no matter how great the apparent settlement, the possibility of error in the prediction is always present. When the prediction does not reach so high a standard, we speak of the law as doubtful or uncertain. Farther down is the vanishing point where law does not exist, and must be brought into being, if at all, by an act of free creation.

I wrote these words before I had seen an interesting article by Dr. John C. H. Wu on the "Juristic Philosophy of Mr. Justice Holmes."[17] My thought, it will be seen, is in close approach to theirs. "The prophecies of what the courts will do in fact, and nothing more pretentious," says Holmes, "are what I mean by the

[17] 21 *Mich. L. R.* 523, 530, March, 1923.

law."[18] Dr. Wu develops with acuteness the implications of the statement. "Law is, thus, a matter of prediction. It does not even consist of the rules already recognized and acted on, as Salmond would define it;[19] it consists of the rules which the courts will probably recognize or act on. . . . Psychologically, law is a science of prediction *par excellence*. It concerns primarily our future interest; people do not study cases for pleasure, but generally with a view to anticipating what the courts will do when future cases arise. One constantly refers, it is true, to past cases as so many depositaries of the law, but in the last analysis that is done almost always with the intention of showing that there is sufficient ground for believing that the courts will act in such and such a way in the future." Analysis of right and duty exposes the same core within them. "For legal purposes," says Holmes, *Collected Papers* (p. 313), "a right is only the

[18] 21 *Mich. L. R.* 530, citing Holmes, *Collected Papers*, p. 173.

[19] Salmond, *Jurisprudence*, p. 9, 4th ed.

hypostasis of prophecy—the imagination of a substance supporting the fact that the public force will be brought to bear upon those who do things said to contravene it—just as we talk of the force of gravitation accounting for the conduct of bodies in space." "A legal duty so called is nothing but a prediction that if a man does or omits certain things, he will be made to suffer in this or that way by judgment of the court."[20]

I know there is a vagueness in all this that may dissatisfy the seeker for inflexible categories, clean-cut and definite compartments, ticketed and labeled and capable of being recognized at sight. The quest is constant and persistent, but it is doomed to disappointment. I do not need to enter into a discussion of the meaning of truth itself.[21] The reality that is absolute and unconditioned may exist, but man must know it, if at all, through its manifestations in the conditioned and the relative. Pragmatism is at least a working rule by which truth is to be

[20] *Collected Papers,* p. 169.
[21] James, *Pragmatism;* James, *The Nature of Truth.*

tested, and its attainment known.[22] If philosophy
has not yet been able to penetrate the mystery
of substance, if it has not yet been able to tell
us wherein consists the identity of things,[23]
we ought not to feel surprise that it is still
baffled by the products of conceptual thought,
the never ending struggle over universals, their
content and identity.[24] I am not concerned to
inquire whether back of these uniformities which
have their flower and fruit in judgments, there
may be others still higher and broader, revelations of a social order, norms of right and justice, to which the lower and narrower uniformities must conform, and after which they must be
patterned, if they are to be effective and endur-
ing. I doubt whether these types or patterns,
except to the extent that they are consistent with
statute or decision, should receive the name of

[22] In this sense at least, we may say with Comte:
"Tout est relatif, voilà le seul principe absolu" (Windelband, *Introduction to Philosophy*, p. 38; *cf. ibid.*, pp.
45, 179).

[23] Windelband, *supra*, pp. 52, 55, *et seq.*

[24] Windelband, p. 186.

law, though in the view of Duguit and others,[25] statute or decision is law only to the extent that it is a sharer in their essence, an expression of their spirit. "The more I advance in age," writes Duguit,[26] "and seek to penetrate the problem of law, the more I am convinced that law is not a creation of the state, that it exists without the state, that the notion of law is altogether independent of the state, and that the rule of law imposes itself on the state as it does upon individuals." Legal obligation, as he views it, is not an "obligation modifying the individual will, but an obligation purely social, that is to say, of such a nature that if it is not satisfied, it produces a disturbance of equilibrium in the constituent elements of the social group, and, as a consequence, a social reaction, that is to say, a spontaneous effort to reëstablish equilibrium."[27] Speculations of this kind, however interesting in themselves, are alien, after all, to the subject of

[25] *Cf.* H. Krabbe, *The Modern Idea of the State.*
[26] *Traité de droit constitutionnel,* 2d ed., vol. I, p. 33
[27] Vol. I, p. 20; *cf.* pp. 87, 88.

our study. If there is any law which is back of
the sovereignty of the state, and superior thereto,
it is not law in such a sense as to concern the
judge or the lawyer, however much it concerns
the statesman or the moralist. The courts are
creatures of the state and of its power, and while
their life as courts continues, they must obey
the law of their creator.[28] This seems to be
recognized by Duguit himself. He draws a distinction between "la règle de droit normative,"
and "la règle de droit constructive," which comes
pretty close to throwing his whole theory over-
board except for the student of statecraft or of
ethics. A normative rule or juridical norm exists
when the mass of the individuals composing the
social group comprehend and admit that a reaction against the violators of the rule can be
socially organized.[29] A constructive rule is a rule
established to assure the enforcement, so far as
possible, of a normative rule,[30] and implies the

[28] *Cf.* Sabine & Shepard, Introduction to H. Krabbe's
The Modern Idea of the State, p. xlv.
[29] *Traité de droit constitutionnel*, vol. I, p. 36; also
p. 41.
[30] P. 38.

existence of a state.[31] "The great mass of our positive laws," he writes[32] "are composed of constructive or technical rules which imply a more or less developed political organization. They are addressed in reality to government and its agents. . . . Although they imply the existence of a state, they may be simply customary. They are obligatory for government and for the representatives of government." The norms are little more than those prevailing habits and convictions which cannot safely be ignored if law in its administration is to win obedience and respect.[33]

[31] P. 39.

[32] P. 41.

[33] This subject is well treated by A. R. Lord, *The Principles of Politics*, pp. 69, 70, 81, 91, 193, 197, 278, 295.

"The sovereign does not create justice in an ethical sense, to be sure, and there may be cases in which it would not dare to deny that justice for fear of war or revolution. Sovereignty is a question of power, and no human power is unlimited. Carino v. Insular Government of the Philippine Islands, 212 U. S. 449, 458. But from the necessary point of view of the sovereign and its organs whatever is enforced by it as law is enforced as the expression of its will. Kawananakoa v. Polyblank, 205 U. S. 349, 353" (Holmes, J., in the *Western Maid*, 257 U. S. 432). *Cf.* Haldane, *The Reign of Relativity*, p. 378.

"I have no difficulty in acknowledging," he continues,[34] "that a juridical norm taken by itself and independently of the means of putting it in force, is a view of the mind rather than a concrete reality. One would find with difficulty either in primitive or in civilized societies juridical norms unaccompanied by legal instrumentalities for putting them in force, created either by custom or by the written law. One can cite the 'leges imperfectae' of Roman law. But aside from the fact that they were very rare, it seems that they were accompanied in one way or another at least by indirect sanctions. However that may be, almost always the normative rule is enveloped in constructive rules, which create an organization, sometimes altogether rudimentary, sometimes very developed and very scientific, and which open up instrumentalities tending to sanction directly or indirectly the obligations negative or positive resulting from the norm." "Normative rules" cease to be law for the advocate or the judge when they are over-

[34] Vol. I, p. 134.

ridden by "constructive rules." They are then merely standards or ideals which in time may win their way. Advocate or judge must reject them as law till their day of triumph has been reached, and the state is ready to support them through its courts and other agencies with the sanction of its power.

A principle or rule of conduct so established as to justify a prediction with reasonable certainty that it will be enforced by the courts if its authority is challenged, is, then, for the purpose of our study, a principle or rule of law. In speaking of principles and rules of conduct, I include those norms or standards of behavior which, if not strictly rules or principles, since they have not been formally declared in statute or decision,[35] are none the less the types or patterns to which statute or decision may be expected to conform. All that I mean to deny them is a potency superior to that of the established organs of the state. They have their roots in the

[35] Ehrlich, *Grundlegung der Soziologie des Rechts*, p. 368.

customary forms and methods of business and of fellowship, the prevalent convictions of equity and justice, the complex of belief and practice which we style the *mores* of the day. They may lack an official *imprimatur*,[36] but this will not always hinder us from resting securely on the assumption that the omission will be supplied when occasion so demands.[37] Unless and until our expectation is disappointed, a standard or rule or principle so verified is treated as law in the governance of conduct, and may fairly be characterized as law in the governance of speech. The uniformity that issues in a reasonable prediction of continuance is the uniformity obeyed.

I have not embarked on this inquiry as a mere exercise in dialectics. I am persuaded that at the root of any satisfactory philosophy of growth, there must be an understanding of what it is that is to grow, a philosophy of genesis or birth. We

[36] Holland, *Elements of Jurisprudence*, p. 54.

[37] *Cf.* Ehrlich, *Grundlegung der Soziologie des Rechts*, p. 8. For illustrations of customs recently recognized by a court as invested with the force of law, see McKee v. Gratz, 260 U. S. 127, 136, and Walker v. Gish, 260 U. S. 447, 450.

must get away at one extreme from the notion that law is fixed and immutable, that the conclusion which the judge declares, instead of being itself a more or less tentative hypothesis, an approximate formulation of a uniformity and an order inductively apprehended, has a genuine preëxistence, that judgment is a process of discovery, and not in any degree a process of creation. This is the extreme of which Blackstone is the most eminent exponent. On the other hand, we must avoid another extreme, which, if not the view of Austin, is a version of his thought, or perhaps a perversion, much developed by his successors,—the conception of law as a series of isolated dooms, the general merged in the particular, the principle dethroned and the instance exalted as supreme. Each extreme has a tendency, though for a different reason, to stifle the creative element. The one teaches the lesson that there is nothing to create. The other teaches the lesson that the thing created is a finality, and that the duty is to reproduce. The apotheosis of *stare decisis* is the result. The judgment is the thing. There is no law behind it or apart from it. Let us worship at the shrine of the literal and the actual. What has been held has a significance so unique that, in addition to accepting it as a datum, we are to accept its logical implications as supplying the sole instruments of advance. Between these two extremes we have the conception of law as a body of rules and principles and standards which in their extension to new combinations of events are to be sorted, selected, moulded, and adapted in subordination to an end. A process of trial and error brings judgments into being. A process of trial and error determines their right to reproduce their kind.

III.

The Growth of Law, and the Methods of Judging.

FROM genesis I pass to growth. In what I have to say I propose to limit myself to growth through the judicial process. There may also, of course, be growth through legislation, but the science of legislation is no part of the field of my inquiry. How does the judge develop and extend the body of uniformities which we have named the law when changing combinations of events make development or extension needful? Is there only one method at his call, or is there a choice of methods, and if so, how do they differ, and what are the principles that are to regulate the choice between them? Some reasoned knowledge of these things is an important part of our equipment for service at the bar or on the bench. I confess that only late in life did a sense of its importance come to me. While I was in practice at the bar, I tried to find the pertinent authority, and fit it to the case at hand. I was not much concerned whether it was right if I was sure that it was pertinent, and I had a blind faith which persisted in the face of reverses and discouragements, that if its pertinency was established, if it fitted well and truly, the courts would follow it inexorably to the limit of its logic. I learned by sad experience that they failed, now and again, to come out where I expected. I thought, however, in my simplicity that they had missed the road or carelessly misread the signposts; the divagations never had the aspect of willful adventures into the land of the unknown. The problem stood before me in a new light when I had to cope with it as judge. I found that the creative element was greater than I had fancied; the forks in the road more frequent; the signposts less complete. "We are not bound to believe," says Pound,[1] "that they [the judges] make legal precepts and set up

[1] *Interpretations of Legal History*, p. 127.

legal institutions out of whole cloth. Except as an act of Omnipotence, creation does not mean the making of something out of nothing. Creative activity takes materials and gives them form so that they may be put to uses for which the materials unformed are not adapted." Some cases, of course, there are where one route and only one is possible. They are the cases where the law is fixed and settled. They make up in bulk what they lack in interest. Other cases present a genuine opportunity for choice—not a choice between two decisions, one of which may be said to be almost certainly right and the other almost certainly wrong, but a choice so nicely balanced that when once it is announced, a new right and a new wrong will emerge in the announcement. I do not mean, of course, that even in those cases, the preference is blind or arbitrary. The balance is swayed, not by gusts of fancy, but by reason. The judge who chooses believes with varying intensity of conviction that he has chosen well and wisely. None the less, even in his mind, there has been a genuine, not merely a nominal alternative. There have been two paths, each open, though leading to different goals. The fork in the road has not been neutralized for the traveler by a barrier across one of the prongs with the label of "no thoroughfare." He must gather his wits, pluck up his courage, go forward one way or the other, and pray that he may be walking, not into ambush, morass, and darkness, but into safety, the open spaces, and the light.

In the opening pages of his book on pragmatism,[2] William James quotes a remark of Chesterton's to the effect that the most important thing about a man is his philosophy. The more I reflect about a judge's work, the more I am impressed with the belief that this, if not true for everyone, is true at least for judges. Of course, it is easy to misunderstand such a statement—to press it too far—and to make it an untruth. Ignorance or indolence may take shelter behind generalities of this kind. Lawyers who are unwilling to study the law as it is, may discover,

[2] James, *Pragmatism*, pp. 1, 2.

as they think, that study is unnecessary; sentiment or benevolence or some vague notion of social welfare becomes the only equipment needed. I hardly need to say that this is not my point of view. Nothing can take the place of rigorous and accurate and profound study of the law as already developed by the wisdom of the past. This is the raw material which we are to mould. Without it, no philosophy will amount to much, any more than a theory of aesthetics will help the sculptor who would mould the statue without clay. Nine-tenths, perhaps more, of the cases that come before a court are predetermined—predetermined in the sense that they are predestined—their fate preëstablished by inevitable laws that follow them from birth to death. The range of free activity is relatively small. We may easily seem to exaggerate it through excess of emphasis. None the less, those are the fields where the judicial function gains its largest opportunity and power. Those are the fields, too, where the process is of the largest interest. Given freedom of choice, how shall the choice be guided? Complete freedom—unfettered and undirected—there never is. A thousand limitations—the product some of statute, some of precedent, some of vague tradition or of an immemorial technique,—encompass and hedge us even when we think of ourselves as ranging freely and at large. The inscrutable force of professional opinion presses upon us like the atmosphere, though we are heedless of its weight. Narrow at best is any freedom that is allotted to us. How shall we make the most of it in service to mankind?

A year or so ago, I was rash enough to publish some lectures on "The Nature of the Judicial Process" as I found it working in our law. I attempted then a fourfold division of the forces to be obeyed and the methods to be applied. The division, as I was at pains to point out, involved some overlapping of the lines,[3] but it seemed, for purposes of rough classification, to be helpful

[3] *Nature of the Judicial Process*, p. 51; *cf.* Professor Cohen's Introduction, pp. 29, 30, Tourtoulon's *Philosophy in the Development of Law*, vol. XIII, Modern Legal Philosophy Series.

and perhaps sufficient. I adhere to it now, in obedience to the law of parsimony of effort, since it is easier to follow the beaten track than it is to clear another. In doing this, I shall be treading in the footsteps of my predecessors, and illustrating the process that I am seeking to describe, since the power of precedent, when analyzed, is the power of the beaten track. Our fourfold division separates the force of logic or analogy, which gives us the method of philosophy; the force of history, which gives us the historical method, or the method of evolution; the force of custom, which yields the method of tradition; and the force of justice, morals and social welfare, the *mores* of the day, with its outlet or expression in the method of sociology. No doubt there is ground for criticism when logic is represented as a method in opposition to the others. In reality, it is a tool that cannot be ignored by any of them.[4] The thing that counts chiefly is the nature of the premises. We may take as our premise some preëstablished concep-

[4] Cohen, *supra.*

tion or principle or precedent, and work it up by an effort of pure reason to its ultimate development, the limit of its logic. We may supplement the conception or principle or precedent by reference to extrinsic sources, and apply the tool of our logic to the premise as thus modified or corrected. The difference between the function of logic in the one case and in the other is in reality a difference of emphasis. The tool is treated on the one hand as a sufficient instrument of growth, and on the other as an instrument to coöperate with others. The principle of division is a difference, not of kind, but of degree. With this reservation, the fourfold classification of methods has sufficient correspondence with realities to supply a basis of distinction. The judicial process will not be rationalized until these methods have been valued, their functions apportioned, their results appraised, until a standard has been established whereby choice may be directed between one method and another. We may find the subject to be such that the hope to rationalize it fully, at all events in our day, will have to be dismissed as futile. That is not a reason for refusing to do the best we can.

Now, the analysis of the forces and methods which do in fact govern the decision of the doubtful case is the task of that part of the philosophy of law which deals with development and growth, and the fixing of the standards by which choice should be directed is the task of that part which deals with functions and with ends. In the nature of things, the latter branch of the inquiry is the more delicate and uncertain. No recipe for the mingling of the ingredients has yet been formulated. Perhaps none can be formulated, unless it be as a hint, an illustration, a suggestion. But if we were never to reach the stage of synthesis, the process of analysis would of itself be worth the labor. The mere recognition of the truth that there are more methods to be applied than one, that there is more than one string to harp upon, is in itself a forward step and a long one upon the highway to salvation. We must spread the gospel, writes Professor Powell in a private letter from which I quote with his permission, we must "spread the gospel that there is no gospel that will save us from the pain of choosing at every step."[5] There are times when precedents seem to lead to harsh or bizarre conclusions, at war with social needs. The law assumes the aspect of a scholastic exercise, divorced from the realities of life. In such junctures, judges would do well to keep before them as a living faith that a choice of methods is theirs in the shaping of their judgments. I do not mean to say that any one method has ever been consistently pursued in a whole department of the law to the exclusion of the others. Interaction has been inevitable, even when unconscious. I mean that particular causes have been determined and particular rules established or extended in submission to a technique which was supposed to coerce when it was intended to advise. We have not yet been able to orient ourselves with all our opportunities for experiment in centuries of experience. We do not know

[5] *Cf.* Dewey, *Human Nature and Conduct*, pp. 239, 241.

where we should face. Judges march at times to pitiless conclusions under the prod of a remorseless logic which is supposed to leave them no alternative. They deplore the sacrificial rite. They perform it, none the less, with averted gaze, convinced as they plunge the knife that they obey the bidding of their office. The victim is offered up to the gods of jurisprudence on the altar of regularity. One who seeks examples may be referred to Dean Pound's illuminating paper on "Mechanical Jurisprudence."[6] I suspect that many of these sacrifices would have been discovered to be needless if a sounder analysis of the growth of law, a deeper and truer comprehension of its methods, had opened the priestly ears to the call of other voices. We should know, if thus informed, that magic words and incantations are as fatal to our science as they are to any other. Methods, when classified and separated, acquire their true bearing and perspective as means to an end, not as ends in themselves. We seek to find peace of mind in the word, the

[6] 8 *Col. L. R.* 603.

formula, the ritual. The hope is an illusion.[7] We think we shall be satisfied to match the situation to the rule, and, finding correspondence, to declare it without flinching. Hardly is the ink dry upon our formula before the call of an unsuspected equity—the urge of a new group of facts, a new combination of events—bids us blur and blot and qualify and even, it may be, erase. The counterdrive—the tug of emotion—is too strong to be resisted. What Professor Dewey says of problems of morals[8] is true, not in like degree, but, none the less, in large measure, of the deepest problems of the law; the situations which they present, so far as they are real problems, are almost always unique. There is nothing that can relieve us of "the pain of choosing at every step."

I do not underrate the yearning for mechanical and formal tests. They are possible and use-

[7] Holmes, "The Path of the Law," *Collected Papers*, pp. 167, 180; Pound, *Criminal Justice in Cleveland*, p. 562.

[8] *Reconstruction in Philosophy; Human Nature and Conduct*.

ful in zones upon the legal sphere. The pain of choosing is the pain of marking off such zones from others. It is a pain we must endure, for uniformity of method will carry us upon the rocks. The curse of this fluidity, of an ever shifting approximation, is one that law must bear, or other curses yet more dreadful will be invited in exchange. We can hardly hope to have it otherwise when we see how law develops. There are some thoughts in Keynes's recent book on the logic of probabilities which have their significance in this connection for lawyer and for judge. "In most branches of academic logic," says Keynes, "such as the theory of the syllogism or the geometry of ideal space, all the arguments aim at demonstrative certainty. They claim to be *conclusive*. But many other arguments are rational and claim some weight without pretending to be certain. In Metaphysics, in Science, and in Conduct, most of the arguments upon which we habitually base our rational beliefs, are admitted to be inconclusive in a greater or less degree. Thus for a philosophical treatment of these branches of knowledge, the study of probability is required. The course which the history of thought has led Logic to follow has encouraged the view that doubtful arguments are not within its scope. But in the actual exercise of reason we do not wait on certainty, or deem it irrational to depend on a doubtful argument. If logic investigates the general principles of valid thought, the study of arguments, to which it is rational to attach *some* weight, is as much a part of it as the study of those which are demonstrative."[9] This is a distinction to be taken to heart by all of us who have a part in the development of law. We tend sometimes, in determining the growth of a principle or a precedent, to treat it as if it represented the outcome of a quest for certainty. That is to mistake its origin. Only in the rarest instances, if ever, was certainty either possible or expected. The principle or the precedent was the outcome of a quest for probabilities. Principles and precedents,

[9] J. M. Keynes, *A Treatise on Probability*, p. 3. *Cf.* Charles S. Pierce, *Chance, Love and Logic*, p. 64.

thus generated, carry throughout their lives the birthmarks of their origin. They are in truth provisional hypotheses, born in doubt and travail, expressing the adjustment which commended itself at the moment between competing possibilities.[10] We need not wonder that there is disappointment, ending in rebellion, when the effort is made to deduce the absolute and eternal from premises which in their origin were relative and transitory. The more we study law in its making, at least in its present stages of development, the more we gain the sense of a gradual striving toward an end, shaped by a logic which, eschewing the quest for certainty, must be satisfied if its conclusions are rooted in the probable.[11]

[10] *Cf.* Holmes, vol. I, *Continental Legal History Series*, p. 46.

[11] I have been interested to find that Tourtoulon in his work on *Philosophy in the Development of Law* (recently translated in the Modern Legal Philosophy Series) has seen these variable and tentative forces working throughout history. "The philosophy of chance," he says (p. 634, vol. XIII, Modern Legal Philosophy Series), "seems to me the most natural conclusion of a philosophy of legal history. It substitutes the search for

THE METHODS OF JUDGING

I have spoken in generalities. Let me point
my meaning by example. My search is for a case
where there was an opportunity for diverse
methods, and where the choice controlled the
outcome. Perhaps as good a one as any is the
decision of the Court of Appeals of New York
in Ives v. The South Buffalo Railway Co.[12]
That is the case, you will remember, where
the Workmen's Compensation Act of 1910 was
adjudged unconstitutional. The act required an
employer to contribute to an insurance fund for
the benefit of employees injured in the course
of their employment. Property was held to have
been taken without due process when a contribution was thus levied regardless of the employer's fault. Now, here was a case where a
choice of methods was possible. It is quite aside

probability for the search for certainty. It shows the
complexity of causes where others wish to see only a de-
ceptive simplicity. It permits man to utilize, so far as possible, his own ignorance. It inspires a salutary scepticism,
not that of negation, but that of prudence; the kindly,
scrupulous and searching scepticism which might well
be the best instrument of progress for humanity."

[12] 201 N. Y. 271.

from my purpose to inquire whether the choice as made was right. The decision has been superseded by amendment of the constitution so far as it involves a problem in the constitutional law of the state.[13] It has been rejected by the Supreme Court of the United States in so far as it involves a problem in the constitutional law of the nation.[14] What interests me at the moment is that a problem in the choice of methods lay back of the problem of law, and determined its solution. On the one hand, the right of property, as it was known to the fathers of the republic, was posited as permanent and absolute. Impairment was not to be suffered except within narrow limits of history and precedent. No experiment was to be made along new lines of social betterment. The image was a perfect sphere. The least dent or abrasion was a subtraction from its essence. Given such premises, the conclusion is inevitable. The statute becomes an illegitimate assault upon rights

[13] Southern Pacific Ry. Co. v. Jensen, 215 N. Y. 514.
[14] N. Y. C. R. R. Co. v. White, 243 U. S. 188.

assured to the individual against the encroachments of society. The method of logic or philosophy is at work in all its plenitude. The opposing view, if it is to be accepted, must be reached through other avenues of approach. The right which the assailants of the statute posit as absolute or permanent is conceived of by the supporters of the statute as conditioned by varying circumstances of time and space and environment and degree. The limitations appropriate to one stage of development may be inadequate for another. Not logic alone, but logic supplemented by the social sciences becomes the instrument of advance. We may frame our conclusions for convenience as universal propositions. We are to remember that in truth they are working hypotheses.[15] The catalogue of causes will be incomplete if the material and the formal and the efficient are enumerated to the exclusion of the final. The truth is not always to be reached by looking back to the beginning and

[15] *Cf.* Dewey, *Human Nature and Conduct,* "The Nature of Principles," p. 239.

deducing from the source. The end may be frustrated unless we look forward to the goal.

The same divergent strains, the same opposition in the selected method, will be found in other cases which have become landmarks of the law. To go back but a few years or months, we may trace it in such decisions as the rent cases,[16] the case of the Arizona statute limiting the remedy of injunction in controversies between capital and labor,[17] and the minimum wage case.[18] One group erects within the mind a norm or standard of reasonable or traditional immunity, and from that deduces a conclusion as to the minimum acceptable in a given situation. The other group seeks the standard, not so much within, as without, and "among the important facts deserving consideration" includes "the prevailing public opinion concerning the evils and the remedy."[19] Of course, in the end, the differ-

[16] Block v. Hirsch, 256 U. S. 135; Marcus Brown Holding Co. v. Feldman, 256 U. S. 170.

[17] Truax v. Corrigan, 257 U. S. 312.

[18] Adkins v. The Children's Hospital of the District of Columbia, 261 U. S. 525.

[19] Brandeis, J., in Truax v. Corrigan, *supra.*

ence is a difference of degree. No absolutist is so intransigent as to assert that there can be literal adherence to a standard of equality or liberty. Some compromise is inevitable between liberty and license, between uniformity and diversity. The necessity for exceptions being conceded, the important thing is to determine the principle that shall govern their allowance. Shall we look for it within ourselves, in some mental pattern of an ideal community? Shall we look for it in the past, admitting no encroachment not sanctified by time? Or shall we look for it in the needs of the present, in "the exigencies of social life?"[20] Shall our standard be a metaphysical conception, or an historic datum, or a living need? As you give one answer or the other, you will reach different results. The trouble often arises from assuming that one method is supreme, from assuming that the truth or apparent truth yielded to us by one of them is to be accepted

[20] Vander-Eycken, *Méthode Positive de l'interprétation juridique*, p. 401; see my *Nature of the Judicial Process*, p. 122; Pound, 44 *Reports Am. Bar Assn.* for 1919, p. 457.

without checking it and testing it by the truth yielded by the others. We are not to bow down before our metaphysical conception or our historic datum, and shut our eyes to living needs, and yet we are not to find a living need in every gust of fancy that would blow to earth the patterns of history and reason.[21]

My illustrations have been taken from the field of public law, but the field of private law also will yield one crop or another with the method which the husbandman applies. What are the rights of a stranger to a contract? Shall the development of the subject be guided by the image of the perfect sphere? Shall indentation or protuberance, no matter how convenient, be forbidden as deformities? Clinging to the conception of a contractual tie, shall we say that the parties linked together by the tie, and no one else, shall have a remedy in the courts when the tie has wrongfully been severed? The English courts have been faithful to the preëstab-

[21] *Cf*. Meyer v. Nebraska, 262 U. S. 390; Bartels v. Iowa, 262 U. S. 404.

lished conception, and have permitted no conclusion at war with logical deduction. At all events, the deviations, if any, have been few and doubtful. We in the United States have been readier to subordinate logic to utility, so that the remedies of third parties, beneficiaries of a contract, at first grudgingly allowed, are now multiplying and expanding.[22] The development is merely a phase of the assault, now extending along the entire line, upon the ancient citadel of privity. In New York, there is a remedy in tort, regardless of privity, against the negligent manufacturer, where the subject of the manufacture is likely to be dangerous to life.[23] The things classified as dangerous have been steadily extended with a corresponding extension of the application of the remedy. They began with Thomas v. Winchester[24] and the sale of poisons. They have been widened till they include a scaffold[25] or an automobile[26] or even pies and cakes

[22] *Nature of the Judicial Process*, p. 99.
[23] MacPherson v. Buick Mfg. Co., 217 N. Y. 382.
[24] 6 N. Y. 397.
[25] Devlin v. Smith, 89 N. Y. 470.
[26] MacPherson v. Buick Mfg. Co., *supra*.

when nails and other foreign substances have supplied ingredients not mentioned in the recipes of cook books. From the field of torts, exceptions have spread to other fields on the borderland between tort and contract. Lack of privity will not defeat a right of action against a public weigher who certifies a weight at the order of one with the intent that the certificate shall guide the conduct of another.[27] Even in the United States, however, the current is not uniform. Recent decisions in Massachusetts have enforced the requirement of privity where a manufacturer has been sued by the victim of his negligence.[28] Logic and utility still struggle for the mastery.

In this analysis of the principles that shape the genesis and growth of law, I have striven to warn against the notion that any one of them is sovereign, that any one is invariably to be preferred over the others, that logic must always yield to history, or history to custom, or all to justice or utility as constituents of the social

[27] Glanzer v. Shepard, 233 N. Y. 236.
[28] Pitman v. Lynn Gas & Electric Co., 235 Mass. 322

welfare. Even if it be true that social welfare is the final test, "certainty and order are themselves constituents of the welfare which it is our business to discover."[29] My effort till now has been to analyze rather than to choose, to show that varying methods lead to varying results, not to fix the criteria by which preference is to be governed. The principles that are to determine choice must be formulated by that branch of the philosophy of law which is concerned with ends and functions. We have (let us assume) a group of precedents before us covering fields more or less analogous to the field of the problem to be solved. Sometimes the analogies are competitive. Shall we adopt this one or that? Shall we press forward on one line or on another? If logic is to be our guide, shall it be the logic of one analogy, the deduction from one principle, or the logic and the deduction that have their origin in others? You must not think of the choice as solely between logic and history, or logic and custom, or logic and justice. Often

[29] See my *Nature of the Judicial Process*, p. 67.

the strife will be one of civil war between the logics, the analogies, themselves, with social utility stepping in as the arbiter between them. A choice must be made. In order that it may be made intelligently, two things must be known. Given a problem whether the directive force of a principle or a rule or a precedent is to be exerted along this path or along that, we must know how the principle or the rule or the precedent is functioning, and what is the end which ought to be attained. The two inquiries coalesce. Let me speak first of ends or aims, reserving till later what I may say of function, in so far as the two inquiries are distinct.

IV.

The Function and the Ends of Law

"MAKING or finding law, call it what you will, presupposes," says Pound,[1] "a mental picture of what one is doing, and of why he is doing it." If conflicting methods are applicable, our understanding of the significance of the process will regulate the preference. To state the ends of law would be the subject matter of a treatise. I shall not attempt to crowd the treatment within the limits of a lecture. Lack of time is a sufficient excuse, though I should be prepared to plead others, if others were required. My present purpose will be attained if I arouse in you a sense of the bond between law and its philosophy. In the analysis of ends, the most fruitful generalizations yet reached, at least in Anglo-American law, are those of Roscoe Pound. Certain branches of the law call in conspicuous

[1] *Introduction to Philosophy*, p. 59.

measure for certainty and order, for an administration of justice that is strict and in a sense mechanical. He places here inheritance and succession, definition of interests in property and the conveyance thereof, matters of commercial law, and the creation incidents and transfers of obligations.[2] If he were to apportion methods in accordance with the scheme of division which I have followed, he would say that the methods applicable here are those of logic, history, and custom. Other branches of the law are better served where flexible standards, capable of being individualized to meet the needs of varying conditions, supersede the rigid rule with its mechanical application. He places here the law of torts, of public utilities, of fiduciary relations, and generally those branches that deal immediately with conduct.[3] If he were to apportion methods in accordance with my division, he would give precedence in this sphere to the method of sociology. A recent paper by Professor Sunderland

[2] *Introduction to Philosophy of Law*, p. 139; *cf* Stammler, 21 *Mich. L. R.* 873.

[3] Pp. 138, 140.

of the University of Michigan develops with much suggestive power the distinction between substantive law and the law of procedure in respect of their several claims to flexibility and to certainty.[4] No doubt, there is a borderland, a penumbra, where methods blend into one another without perceptible division. The apportionment of the relative value of certainty on the one side and justice on the other, of adherence to logic and advancement of utility, involves an appraisement of the social interest which each is capable of promoting. That is a calculus which has not yet been definitively made by any master of juristic theory.[5] Fruitful and penetrating suggestions have been contributed by Pound,[6]

[4] 5 *Am. Law School Rev.*, p. 73, Mar., 1923; 29 *W. Va. Law Quart.* 77.

[5] Albertsworth, "Program of Sociological Jurisprudence," VIII *Am. Bar Assn. Jour.* 393, 396; *cf.* Bentham, *Principles of Morals and Legislation;* Windelband, *Introduction to Philosophy,* 227, 229; Vander-Eycken, *Méthode positive de l'interprétation juridique;* Tourtoulon, *Philosophy in the Development of Law,* XIII Modern Legal Philosophical Series, p. 479, 486.

[6] Pound, "A Study of Social Interests," vol. XV, *Papers and Proceedings of American Sociological Society* May, 1921.

but they do not profess to be more than provisional and tentative. Sociological jurisprudence, in the words of Dean Stone, has yet to develop the formulas and principles "which can be taught and expounded so as to make it a methodological guide either to the student of law or to the judge."[7] Its value at present is largely negative.[8] "It warns the judge and the student of law that logic and history cannot and ought not to have full sway when the dynamic judgment is to be rendered. It points out that in the choice of the particular device determining the result—social utility—the *mores* of the times, objectively determined, may properly turn the scale in favor of one against the other."[9] If classification were ever to become complete for any time and place, there is little chance that it would be final. The good of one generation is not always the good of its successor. For the lawyer as for the moralist,

[7] 22 *Col. L. R.* 382, 384.

[8] Albertsworth, *supra*.

[9] Stone, *supra* also 23 *Col. L. R.* 328; *cf.* Lepaulle, "The Function of Comparative Law," 35 *Harv. L. R.* 838.

the generalizations that result from the study of social phenomena are "not fixed rules for deciding doubtful cases, but instrumentalities for their investigation, methods by which the value of past experience is rendered available for present scrutiny of new perplexities."[10] Sociology would petrify with a rigidity more fatal than that of logic, or rather, perhaps, with a logic of its own, if its hypotheses were treated as finalities. "The problem," in the words of Dewey, "is one of continuous, vital readaptation."[11]

In the present state of our knowledge, the estimate of the comparative value of one social interest and another, when they come, two or more of them, into collision, will be shaped for the judge, as it is for the legislator, in accordance with an act of judgment in which many elements coöperate. It will be shaped by his experience of life; his understanding of the prevailing canons of justice and morality; his study of the social

[10] Dewey, *Human Nature and Conduct*, pp. 240, 241.
[11] Dewey, *op. cit.*, p. 240.

sciences; at times, in the end, by his intuitions, his guesses, even his ignorance or prejudice. The web is tangled and obscure, shot through with a multitude of shades and colors, the skeins irregular and broken. Many hues that seem to be simple, are found, when analyzed, to be a complex and uncertain blend. Justice itself, which we are wont to appeal to as a test as well as an ideal, may mean different things to different minds and at different times. Attempts to objectify its standards, or even to describe them, have never wholly succeeded.[12] Aristotle distinguishes between corrective justice (διορθωτικόν), distributive justice (διανεμητικόν), and general justice (τὸ καθόλον δίκαιον).[13] Such a classification does

[12] Gény, *Science et Technique en droit privé positif*, vol. I, pp. 49, 50; vol. II, p. 389, § 171; Gény, *Méthode l'interprétation*, etc., vol. II, pp. 107-110; Vinogradoff, *Historical Jurisprudence*, vol. II, p. 45; Duguit, *Traité de droit constitutionnel*, vol. I, pp. 49-53; H. Spencer, Justice, *The Principles of Ethics*, vol. II, § 272, p. 45; Tourtoulon, *Philosophy in the Development of Law*, vol. XIII, Modern Legal Philosophical Series, pp. 266, 479, 492; also p. 36 of Professor Cohen's Introduction; Pollock, *First Book of Jurisprudence*, p. 30.

[13] Vinogradoff, *Historical Jurisprudence*, vol. II, pp. 45-57.

not carry us far. What we are seeking is not
merely the justice that one receives when his
rights and duties are determined by the law as
it is; what we are seeking is the justice to which
law in its making should conform. Justice in this
sense is a concept by far more subtle and indefi-
nite than any that is yielded by mere obedience
to a rule. It remains to some extent, when all is
said and done, the synonym of an aspiration, a
mood of exaltation, a yearning for what is fine or
high. "Justice," says Stammler in a recent
paper,[14] "is the directing of a particular legal
volition according to the conception of a pure
community." Perhaps we shall even find at times
that when talking about justice, the quality we
have in mind is charity, and this though the one
quality is often contrasted with the other.[15] The
ingredient which sours if left alone, is preserved
by an infusion, sweetening the product without
changing its identity. You may give what re-

[14] 21 *Mich. L. R.* 889.
[15] Tourtoulon, *supra;* Professor Cohen's Introduction,
pp. 36, 39.

cipes you will. A trained sense of taste, approving or rejecting, will pass judgment on the whole.

The precept that emerges from this flux seems barren enough indeed, till the transfiguring process of creation has proved it to be fertile. "You shall not for some slight profit of convenience or utility depart from standards set by history or logic; the loss will be greater than the gain. You shall not drag in the dust the standards set by equity and justice to win some slight conformity to symmetry and order; the gain will be unequal to the loss." This and little more will be found inscribed upon the tables. We shall learn, none the less, that the commandment, jejune and vague upon its face, has unsuspected implications, hidden and unknown energies, that are revealed to the devout, to those who seek in very truth and with all their might to follow and obey. Between these poles there is room for an infinitude of nice adjustments, all swayed in some degree by the attraction of the force that radiates from either end. As new problems arise, equity and justice will direct the mind to solutions which will be found, when they are scrutinized, to be consistent with symmetry and order, or even to be the starting points of a symmetry and order theretofore unknown. Logic and history, the countless analogies suggested by the recorded wisdom of the past, will in turn inspire new expedients for the attainment of equity and justice. We find a kindred phenomenon in literature, alike in poetry and in prose. The search is for the just word, the happy phrase, that will give expression to the thought, but somehow the thought itself is transfigured by the phrase when found. There is emancipation in our very bonds. The restraints of rhyme or metre, the exigencies of period or balance, liberate at times the thought which they confine, and in imprisoning release.

The truth, of course, is that in the development of law, as in other fields of thought, we can never rid ourselves of our dependence upon intuitions or flashes of insight transcending and transforming the contributions of mere experience. "The great historians," says Windelband,[16] "had no need to wait for the experiments and research of our psychophysicists. The psychology they used was that of daily life. It was the knowledge of men, the experience of life, of the common man, coupled with the insight of the genius and the poet. No one has ever yet succeeded in making a science of this psychology of intuitive understanding." What is here said of the historian is true also of the lawyer. A perception, more or less dim, of this truth underlies the remark of Graham Wallas,[17] that in some of the judges of our highest court there should be a touch of the qualities which make the poet. The scrutiny and dissection of social facts may supply us with the data upon which the creative spirit broods, but in the process of creation something is given out in excess of what is taken in. Gény, in his *Science and Technique of Law*, reminds us how this notion of the development of law fits into the general scheme of recent philosophical thought, and in particular with the

[16] *Introduction to Philosophy*, pp. 206, 207.
[17] Wallas, *Our Social Heritage*, p. 194.

philosophy of Bergson and Bergson's school. "It is necessary, they tell us, to complete and correct the rigidity of the intellect by the suppleness of instinct, in a way to auscultate the mystery of the universe by means of a sort of intellectual sympathy."[18] "The new philosophy preaches under the name of 'intuition' a mode of knowledge more subtle than pure intellect, a mode of knowledge which instals itself in the very heart of reality," and penetrates, not from without, but from within.[19] We do not need to become the disciples of any theory of epistemology, Bergson's or any other, to perceive the force of the analogy between the creative process here described, and the process at work in the development of law. The mechanism displays the same diversity of form and parts and combinations.[20] Analysis alternates with synthesis; deduction with induction; reasoning with intuition.

[18] Gény, *Science et Technique en droit privé positif*, vol. I, p. 80, § 26.

[19] Gény, *supra; cf.* Pound, "The Theory of Judicial Decision," 36 *Harv. L. R.* 951.

[20] We have that interaction between impulses and habits which Professor Dewey has recently described in his book on *Human Nature and Conduct.*

The whole in Gény's words[21] is "a procedure extremely complex, and full of delicate nuances, all penetrated with casuistry and dialectics, a constant mixture of analysis and synthesis, in which the *a posteriori* processes which furnish adequate solutions presuppose directions *a priori*, proposed by reason and by will." The handling of examples, of concrete instances, will develop the skill proper to the art. Repetition of the precept without more will yield at best a bungling workman. "The artistic activity exhibits a mutual play of conscious and unconscious processes which can never be rationally explained. . . . The creation is accompanied by conscious criticism, but the positive element of achievement is not a matter of cunning and calculation; it comes as a fortunate chance from the unconscious depths of life."[22] So Pound:[23] "The in-

[21] *Ibid.*, vol. I, p. 211, sec. 67.

[22] Windelband, *op. cit.*, pp. 321, 322. "Si la connaissance du droit est une science, il est permis d'affirmer sans présomption que la manière de l'appliquer constitue véritablement un art" (Ransson, *"Essai sur l'art de juger,"* p. 21).

[23] "The Theory of Judicial Decision," 36 *Harv. L. R.* 952.

stinct of the experienced workman operates with assurance. Innumerable details and minute discriminations have entered into it, and it has been gained by long experience which has made the proper inclusions and exclusions by trial and error until the effective line of action has become a habit." And again:[24] "It is an everyday experience of those who study judicial decisions that the results are usually sound, whether the reasoning from which the results purport to flow is sound or not. The trained intuition of the judge continually leads him to right results for which he is puzzled to give unimpeachable legal reasons." This does not mean in law, any more than in art generally, that the precept is to be condemned as useless. The key that methodology gives us will not release and expose the mystery by the mere turning of the hand. It is perhaps not so much a key as a clew, a something to be worked up and developed by ourselves if we would extract the essence of its virtue.

The analysis of social interests and their rela-

[24] Pp. 9, 51.

tive importance is one of the clews, then, that the lawyer and the judge must utilize in the solution of their problems. The study has developed a science of its own. We may not clarify a subject when we give it a special name, but perhaps, in the eyes of some, we give it added dignity, if the name selected is a hard one. A terminology, recondite enough to satisfy these conditions, has grown up in the field which is the subject of our survey. Philosophers have given the name of axiology, or the science of values, to the study that busies itself with the estimate of comparative values in ethical, social, or aesthetic problems.[25] The conclusions of this science must, from time to time, be appropriated by the judge, yet they must be appropriated subject to restrictions which limit his freedom to accept or to reject. When the legislature has spoken, and declared one interest superior to another, the judge must subordinate his personal or subjective estimate of value to the estimate thus declared. He may not nullify or pervert a

[25] Windelband, *op. cit.*, pp. 209, 217.

statute because convinced that an erroneous axiology is reflected in its terms. Even when the legislature has not spoken, he is to regulate his estimate of values by objective rather than subjective standards, by the thought and will of the community rather than by his own idiosyncrasies of conduct and belief.[26] Often the two standards will be identical. At all events, if the communal thought or will is different, there will be neither statute nor custom nor other external token to declare or define the difference. The judge will then have no standard of value available except his own. In such circumstances, the objective will for him be merged in the subjective; the axiology that is to guide him will be his own and not another's.

We need have no fear in thus subordinating the individual to the community that great minds and great souls will be without an opportunity to reveal themselves. The search, indeed, is for something external, a norm which finds

[26] Cf. H. Krabbe, The Modern Idea of the State, pp. 99, 100.

expression in custom or convictions, but, in the very act of declaring what is found, there springs into being a new norm, a new standard, to which custom and convictions tend thereafter to conform. Who can doubt that courts of equity in enforcing the great principle that a trustee shall not profit by his trust nor even place himself in a position where his private interest may collide with his fiduciary duty, have raised the level of business honor, and kept awake a conscience that might otherwise have slumbered? Penetrating thoughts on this subject have been contributed by Duguit. The judge is to scrutinize the aggregate of social facts of which "the juridical norm" is to be regarded as a product. Chief among these are "the positive laws, the usages actually obeyed, the economic needs, the aspirations toward the realization of the just."[27] But the scrutiny, though an essential part of his function, is not the whole.[28] The judge interprets the

[27] Duguit, *Traité de droit constitutionnel,* vol. I, pp. 79, 83.
[28] Pp. 80, 83.

social conscience, and gives effect to it in law, but in so doing he helps to form and modify the conscience he interprets. Discovery and creation react upon each other.

I have been trying to give some notion of the kind of problems that must be met by a philosophy concerning itself with the final causes of the law. I have done this merely as a preface, though the preface has been a long one. What I have wished to lead up to is the bearing of such a philosophy upon the problems that must be met in practice by the lawyer or the judge. In emphasizing the importance of its aid, I have not meant, of course, to convey the suggestion that, left alone, it is all-sufficient. Resort to a philosophy of law in the development of rules and principles presupposes knowledge of the principles and rules which it is our business to develop. Here, as so often, the right word is said by Holmes. "When a man," says Holmes, "has a working knowledge of his business, he can spend his leisure better than in reading all the reported cases he has time for. They are apt to

be only the small change of legal thought."[29]
Many things must be learned as facts in law as
in other sciences. They are the coin which we
must have in our pocket if we are to pay our
way with legal tender. Until we are provided
with a plentiful supply of it, we shall do better
to stay at home, and not go forth upon our
journey. I assume, then, what Holmes calls a
working knowledge of the business. We must
talk as one lawyer to another, or we shall be
talking at cross-purposes. When this common
ground is gained, we shall not go very far before
beginning to philosophize.

Let me assume a case where authority is silent.
You, gentlemen, or as many of you as may be
lucky enough to receive a retainer, are the lawyers. I am the distracted judge. You have ran-
sacked the digests, the cyclopaedias, the trea-
tises, the law reviews. The decision on all fours
which counsel love to produce with a latent note
of triumph, cowing with authority the sceptic

[29] *Introduction to a General Survey of Continental
Legal History,* vol. I, Continental Legal History Series,
p. xlvi.

on the bench, this buried treasure of the law books, refuses to come forth. The vigils and the quest yield at most a few remote analogies, which can be turned as easily to the service of one side as to the service of the other. What are you going to do to persuade? What am I going to do to decide? Perhaps we shall, neither of us, be fully conscious of the implications of the process. Much that goes on in the mind is subconscious or nearly so. But if, when the task is finished, we ask ourselves what we have done, we shall find, if we are frank in the answer, that with such equipment as we have, we have been playing the philosopher.

We had in my court a year or more ago a case that points my meaning.[80] A boy was bathing in a river. He climbed upon a springboard which projected from a bank. As he stood there, at the end of the board, poised for his dive into the stream, electric wires fell upon him, and swept him to his death below. In the suit for damages that followed, competitive analogies were in-

[80] Hynes v. N. Y. Central R. R. Co., 231 N. Y. 229.

voked by counsel for the administratrix and counsel for the railroad company, the owner of the upland. The administratrix found the analogy that suited her in the position of travelers on a highway. The boy was a bathèr in navigable waters; his. rights were not lessened because his feet were on the board. The owner found the analogy to its liking in the position of a trespasser on land. The springboard, though it projected into the water, was, none the less, a fixture, and as a fixture it was constructively a part of the land to which it was annexed. The boy was thus a trespasser upon land in private ownership; the only duty of the owner was to refrain from wanton and malicious injury; if these elements were lacking, the death must go without requital. Now, the truth is that, as a mere bit of dialectics, these analogies would bring a judge to an impasse. No process of merely logical deduction could determine the choice between them. Neither analogy is precise, though each is apposite. There had arisen a new situation which could not force itself without mutilation into any of the existing moulds. When we find a situation of this kind, the choice that will approve itself to this judge or to that, will be determined largely by his conception of the end of the law, the function of legal liability; and this question of ends and functions is a question of philosophy.

In the case that I have instanced, a majority of the court believed that liability should be adjudged. The deductions that might have been made from preëstablished definitions were subordinated and adapted to the fundamental principles that determine, or ought to determine, liability for conduct in a system of law wherein liability is adjusted to the ends which law should serve.[81] Hynes v. The New York Central Rail Road Co., was decided in May, 1921. Dean Pound's *Introduction to the Philosophy of Law* had not yet been published. It appeared in 1922. In these lectures, he advances a theory of liability which it may be interesting to compare with

[81] *Cf.* F. H. Bohlen, "Mixed Questions of Law a Fact," 72 *Univ. of Penn. L. R.*, pp. 111, 120.

the theory of liability reflected in our decision. "The law," he says,[32] "enforces the reasonable expectations arising out of conduct, relations and situations." I shall leave it to others to say whether the cause of the boy diving from the springboard would be helped or hindered by resort to such a test. This much I cannot doubt. *Some* theory of liability, some philosophy of the end to be served by tightening or enlarging the circle of rights and remedies, is at the root of any decision in novel situations when analogies are equivocal and precedents are silent. As it stands today, the judge is often left to improvise such a theory, such a philosophy, when confronted overnight by the exigencies of the case before him. Often he fumbles about, feeling in a vague way that some such problem is involved, but missing the universal element which would have quickened his decision with the inspiration of a principle. If he lacks an adequate philosophy, he either goes astray altogether, or at best does not rise above the empiricism that pro-

[32] P. 189.

nounces judgment upon particulars. We must learn that all methods are to be viewed not as idols but as tools. We must test one of them by the others, supplementing and reënforcing where there is weakness, so that what is strong and best in each will be at our service in the hour of need. Thus viewing them we shall often find that they are not antagonists but allies.

The truth, indeed, is that many a worker in the law who flies the flag of one school is giving aid and comfort unwittingly to another, and should be flying its flag instead. The historical school of jurisprudence is often contrasted with the sociological school, and there are important elements of difference between them, yet many who profess to use the historical method in the adjudication of a cause are in truth less loyal to the significance of the historical school than those who profess the method of sociology, and look more freely to the prevailing standards of welfare and utility. In the view of the historical school, "it is not the law-giver that makes the law; the folk-spirit does it. The law-giver has only to write down what the spirit of the people dictates. To this end it is necessary that he be adequately instructed by systematic studies as to the true meaning of the folk-spirit."[33] "Law is *not a product of human will*, but is *a common conviction*."[34] In all likelihood the historical school has exaggerated the unconscious, the un-volitional, element in the development of law. If, however, its assumptions be accepted, they exact, not blind reproduction of the past, but searching scrutiny of the present, for law, by the very terms of the hypothesis, is the expression of the convictions of the present, not the convictions of the past. Where then shall we look for the revelations of the folk-spirit if not in the prevailing standards of utility and welfare? We take a false and one-sided view of history when we ignore its dynamic aspects. The year books can teach us how a principle or a rule had its

[33] Stammler, "Fundamental Tendencies in Modern Jurisprudence," 21 *Mich. L. R.* 647.

[34] *Ibid.*, p. 650; *cf.* Duguit, *Traité de droit constitutionnel*, vol. I, pp. 56, 72.

beginnings. They cannot teach us that what was the beginning shall also be the end.

I find again in a recent judgment of my own court the case that points my meaning. We held a little while ago in Oppenheim v. Kridel, 236 N. Y. 156, that a woman, as well as a man, may maintain an action for criminal conversation. The court of intermediate appeal had ruled that the action would not lie. To make out the woman's disability, precedents were cited from the time of Lord Coke. Stress was laid upon pronouncements in those days that a man had a property right in the body of his wife. A wife, it was said, had none in the body of her husband. Stress was laid also upon rulings made in days when the wife was unable, unless the husband joined with her as plaintiff, to sue for any wrong. We did not ignore these precedents, but we held them inconclusive. Social, political, and legal reforms had changed the relations between the sexes, and put woman and man upon a plane of equality. Decisions founded upon the assumption of a bygone inequality were unrelated to present-day realities, and ought not to be permitted to prescribe a rule of life.[35] The historical method was the organon of judgment in each court, but its application led in each to opposite results. One court, in its interpretation of legal history, was satisfied to treat as finalities the precedents of ancient year books. The other found a stream of thought, a tendency, a movement forward to a goal. Which, then, is the truer use of the historical method? Which exhibits the saner and the sounder loyalty? Shall the significance of events be determined by transporting them to our own time and viewing them as if they were the product of our own day and thought, or by viewing them as of the time of their occurrence, the product of their era, the expression of its beliefs and habits?

We need a selective process if history is to be read as history, and not merely as a barren chronicle. The several methods of approach, rightly understood and applied, correct and prove each other. An appeal to origins will be

[35] *Cf.* R. v. Jackson, 1891, 1 Q.B. 671.

futile, their significance perverted, unless tested
and illumined by an appeal to ends. We must
learn to handle our tools, to use our methods and
our processes, not singly, but together. They are
instruments of advance to be employed in combination. The failure to combine them, the use
of this method or that as if one were exclusive
of the other, has been the parent of many
wrongs. Only precariously and doubtfully shall
we arrive at the needed combination without the
understanding that comes of accurate analysis—
the analysis that is the essential preliminary to
any sound and truthful synthesis. "Much will
be gained," says Dean Pound[36] "when courts
have perceived what it is that they are doing,
and are thus enabled to address themselves consciously to doing it the best that they may."
This much, if no more, the study of the philosophy of law will teach us. It will teach the great
commandment, "Thou shalt not make unto thy-
self any graven image—of maxims or formulas

[36] 36 *Harv. L. R.* 959.

to wit."[87] At times, indeed, we shall seem to have learned nothing, and shall wonder whether there was profit in the labor and the sacrifice. We shall say to ourselves that it is vain to seek a sovereign talisman; that the treasure box does not spring open at the magic of a whispered word; that there is no one method of judging, supreme over its competitors, but only a choice of methods changing with the changing problem; and that the choice and the attendant travail, far from being transitory phases of the process, are its inseparable conditions, the primal curse which it must suffer. But this, after all, will itself be a philosophy, and one that, taken to heart, may save us many blunders.

[87] Sir Frederick Pollock, 39 *Law Quarterly Review* 169.

V.

Function and Ends (Continued)
Conclusion

I HAVE shown juristic methods sorted and handled by their users in adaptation to the ends which each is capable of serving. The examples I have given may seem to stress the worth of change, the virtue of flexibility, as contrasted with the worth of certainty. To keep the balance true, let me put before you other cases where certainty was found to be the larger good when mobility was weighed against it. A manufacturer of paper made a contract with the publisher of a newspaper to furnish paper in monthly installments of stated quantities for a stated term of years. During the first three months of the term, the price was fixed in advance. During the residue, it was to be such a price, continuing for such a time, as buyer and seller might agree, subject, however, to the proviso that the price to be named for this undesignated period should not be more than that then charged to large consumers by another manufacturer. When the initial period expired, the buyer demanded monthly deliveries at the price established as the maximum. The seller, refusing to comply with the demand, took the ground that the contract was abortive for the reason that there had been no agreement upon the time during which this price was to continue. The Court of Appeals of New York upheld this position, and ruled that the seller's right was unaffected by his motive.[1] Here was a case where advantage had been taken of the strict letter of a contract to avoid an onerous engagement. Not inconceivably a sensitive conscience would have rejected such an outlet of escape. We thought this immaterial. The court subordinated the equity of a particular situation

[1] Sun Printing & Publishing Co. v. Remington Pulp & Paper Company, 235 N. Y. 338. Of course, a different result may be reached if the omitted term is of subsidiary importance (1 Williston, *Contracts*, § 48), but ordinarily the price to be paid, if reserved for subsequent agreement, is to be ranked as fundamental.

to the overmastering need of certainty in the transactions of commercial life. The end to be attained in the development of the law of contract is the supremacy, not of some hypothetical, imaginary will, apart from external manifestations, but of will outwardly revealed in the spoken or the written word. The loss to business would in the long run be greater than the gain if judges were clothed with power to revise as well as to interpret. Perhaps, with a higher conception of business and its needs,[2] the time will come when even revision will be permitted if it is revision in consonance with established standards of fair dealing, but the time is not yet. In this department of activity, the current axiology still places stability and certainty in the forefront of the virtues. "The field is one where the law should hold fast to fundamental conceptions of contract and of duty, and follow them with loyalty to logical conclusions."[3] One could cite other instances without number.[4]

[2] Fosdick, *Christianity and Progress,* p. 111.
[3] Imperator Realty Co. v. Tull, 228 N. Y. 447, 455.
[4] See, *e.g.,* St. Regis Paper Co. v. Hubbs & Hastings

I have spoken thus far of ends. I must give a word to functions. To some extent, the two subjects are coterminous. Our philosophy will tell us the proper function of law in telling us the ends that law should endeavor to attain; but closely related to such a study is the inquiry whether law, as it has developed in this subject or in that, does in truth fulfill its function—is functioning well or ill. The latter inquiry is perhaps a branch of social science, calling for a survey of social facts, rather than a branch of philosophy itself, yet the two subjects converge, and one will seldom be fruitful unless supplemented by the other. "Consequences cannot alter statutes, but may help to fix their meaning."[5] We test the rule by its results.

The point of view seems obvious, yet it wins its way slowly, and with hesitant avowal.[6] A difference has been noted between the attitude of mind of the scientist who studies a problem of

Paper Co., 235 N. Y. 30; Murray v. Cunard S. S. Co., 235 N. Y. 162.

[5] Matter of Rouss, 221 N. Y. 81, 91.

[6] *Cf.* Holmes, *The Common Law*, pp. 1, 2.

the social life of man, and the attitude of mind of scientists in other fields. James Harvey Robinson has a telling passage on the subject in his recent book on *The Mind in the Making* (p. 11). The scientist in other fields asks himself dispassionately, how does the precept work? If he finds that it works ill, he casts it aside as error. The student of society has been disposed to take institutions as he finds them, and, indeed, if he studies them as a judge, he will learn that to a large extent he cannot take them otherwise. Only at long intervals have judges asked themselves the question, How does the precept work? Is it a sensible rule for the governance of mankind? They have not asked the question, for they have looked upon the answer as more or less irrelevant. They have generally been content with the inquiry, Is it a rule that exists? What are its logical presuppositions or its logical developments?

The method of sociology, in stressing ends and functions, involves with growing frequency the approach from other angles. The judge in the effort to decide, the lawyer in the effort to persuade, is driven, as he adopts this method, to test a rule by its results. Of course, there are times, now as in the past, when the inquiry must stop with the answer to the question, Is it a rule that exists? Function becomes important in those cases chiefly where the problem is one of direction or extension. In such circumstances, the choice of a path is blind and unintelligent without a survey of the route which has been traveled and of the place to which the route has brought us.

A recent case in the Supreme Court supplies the needed illustration. The case was a prosecution for murder.[7] The trial judge had charged that the defendant, though attacked with a deadly weapon, was not at liberty to stand his ground if a man of reasonable prudence would have seen a possibility of flight. Support is not lacking for such a statement of the law. The Supreme Court, speaking by Holmes, J., refused to accept a rule so unrelated to normal human

[7] Brown v. U. S., 256 U. S. 335.

conduct under stress of strong emotion. "The law," said Judge Holmes, "has grown, and even if historical mistakes have contributed to its growth, it has tended in the direction of rules consistent with human nature. . . . Detached reflection cannot be demanded in the presence of an uplifted knife. Therefore in this court, at least, it is not a condition of immunity that one in that situation should pause to consider whether a reasonable man might not think it possible to fly with safety or to disable his assailant rather than to kill him." Enough that he reasonably believes the danger to be imminent. The failure to retreat is, indeed, a circumstance to be considered in determining whether the belief is genuine. Given the belief, based on reasonable grounds, immunity is not withdrawn because some other reasonable man might have perceived the possibility of flight. We do not need to inquire whether it is possible to find in this decision a departure from precedents enshrined in the reports. In some states, *e.g.*, New York, the rule is hardened to some extent by the provisions of a statute.[8] What interests us now is not so much the decision itself as its animating spirit. It is built on the assumption that function is perverted if a rule is unrelated to the realities of conduct, and the rule itself is moulded to effect the needed adaptation.

The growing power of this spirit declares itself in many fields. A school of thinkers of increasing weight and number is today stressing the relation between a rule and its effects, between the soundness of the one and the benefits of the other. This has been brought out sharply in the preliminary discussions as to the proposed restatement of the law. We have been reminded that where decisions are conflicting, a choice will be unintelligent unless we are informed which one of the conflicting rules has proved, in its operation, the most workable and useful.[9] Some of the errors of courts have their origin in im-

[8] Penal Law, §§ 42, 1055; People v. Johnson, 139 N. Y. 358; and *cf.* People v. Tomlins, 213 N. Y. 240; People v. Fiori, 123 N. Y. App. Div. 178, 188, 189, 190.

[9] Professor Herman Oliphant, *The Problems of Logical Method,* vol. X, Proceedings of Academy of Political Science in New York, p. 18.

perfect knowledge of the economic and social consequences of a decision, or of the economic and social needs to which a decision will respond. In the complexities of modern life there is a constantly increasing need for resort by the judges to some fact-finding agency which will substitute exact knowledge of factual conditions for conjecture and impression. A study of the opinions of Mr. Justice Brandeis will prove an impressive lesson in the capacity of the law to refresh itself from extrinsic sources, and thus vitalize its growth. His opinions are replete with references to "the contemporary conditions, social, industrial, and political, of the community affected."[10]

Sooner or later, if the demands of social utility are sufficiently urgent, if the operation of an existing rule is sufficiently productive of hardship or inconvenience, utility will tend to triumph. "The view of the legal system as a closed book was never anything but a purely theoretical

[10] Truax v. Corrigan, 257 U. S. 312; *cf* Adams v. Tanner, 244 U. S. 590, 600.

dogma of the schools. Jurisprudence has never been able in the long run to resist successfully a social or economic need that was strong and just."[11] We have a conspicuous illustration in the law of waters in our western states. "Two systems of water law are in force within the United States—the riparian and the appropriation systems."[12] The system first named prevails in thirty-one of the forty-eight states. Its fundamental principle is "that each riparian proprietor has an equal right to make a reasonable use of the waters of the stream, subject to the equal right of the other riparian proprietors likewise to make a reasonable use."[13] Some of the arid states of the west found this system unsuited to their needs. Division of the water "into small quantities among the various water users and on the general principle of equality of right" would be a division "so minute as not to be of

[11] Ehrlich, *Grundlegung der Soziologie des Rechts*, p. 346.

[12] Bannister, "Interstate Rights in Interstate Streams in the Arid West," 36 *Harv. L. R.* 960.

[13] Bannister, *supra.*

advantage to anybody."[14] "It is better in such a region that some have enough and others go without, than that the division should be so minute as to be of no real economic value." The appropriation system is built upon the recognition of this truth. Its fundamental principle is "that the water user who first puts to beneficial use—irrigation, mining, manufacturing, power, household, or other economic use—the water of a stream, acquires thereby the first right to the water, to the extent reasonably necessary to his use, and that he who is the second to put the water of the stream to beneficial use, acquires the second right, a right similar to the first right, but subordinate thereto, and he who is the third to put it to use acquires the third right, a right subordinate to the other two, and so on throughout the entire series of uses."[15] Here we have the conscious departure from a known rule, and the deliberate adoption of a new one, in obedience to the promptings of a social need so obvious

[14] Bannister, *supra*, p. 962.
[15] Bannister, *supra*, p. 961; Wyoming v. Colorado, 259 U. S. 419.

and so insistent as to overrun the ancient channel and cut a new one for itself.

The whole subject of the philosophy of function is, indeed, closely related to the vexed and
perplexing problem of the authority of precedent.
Through one agency or another, either by statute or by decision, rules, however well established, must be revised when they are found
after fair trial to be inconsistent in their work-
ings with an attainment of the ends which law is
meant to serve. The revision is a delicate task,
not to be undertaken by gross or adventurous
hands, lest certainty and order be unduly sacri-
ficed, yet a task also not to be shirked through
timidity or sloth. I have had occasion elsewhere
to indicate a few of the anachronisms that might
be eradicated from the legal system.[16] Many
others could be instanced. Some of this cleansing
of ancient plague spots, the judges ought to do
themselves. To the extent that they are unwilling
or unable, there must be resort to legislation.
The difficulty here is to establish some channel

[16] 35 *Harv. L. R.* 113.

of communication between legislature and courts. The channel is essential, first, that the needs of the courts may be known to the legislature, and, second, that the needs, when known, may be intelligently and promptly met. I have suggested a ministry of justice,[17] though I am not insensible of the imperfections of the plan. More hopeful in its promise of success is the project of the American Law Institute, already outlined in these lectures. The Institute will, of course, be national in scope. None the less, its recommendations may be applied with slight modification to different localities. The local bar associations or the local ministries of justice will thus be supplied with standards by which their own judgment will be guided, their own hesitations overcome, their own diversities corrected. No doubt there are many rules of property or conduct which could not be changed retroactively without hardship or oppression, and this whether wise or unwise in their origin. So far as I am aware, no judge ever thinks of changing them.

[17] 35 *Harv. L. R.* 113.

The picture of the bewildered litigant lured into a course of action by the false light of a decision, only to meet ruin when the light is extinguished and the decision overruled, is for the most part a figment of excited brains. The only rules there is ever any thought of changing are those that are invoked by injustice after the event to shelter and intrench itself. In the rarest instances, if ever, would conduct have been different if the rule had been known and the change foreseen.[18] At times the change means the imposition of a bill of costs that might otherwise have been saved. That is a cheap price to pay for the uprooting of an ancient wrong. One man is made a victim to the extent of a few dollars in return for a readjustment that will save many victims in the future. If change, however, cannot be made through the judicial process, unaided from without, some external agency there must be through which the aid will be supplied. There are times when we can learn whether a rule functions well or ill by compari-

[18] *Cf. The Nature of the Judicial Process*, p. 146.

son with a standard of justice or equity, known, or capable of being known, to us all through a scrutiny of conscience or through appeal to everyday experience. There are times when the manner of its functioning will be unknown without the recorded observations, the collected facts and figures, the patient and systematic studies, of scientists and social workers. "One of the most important functions of any vocational body," says Graham Wallas[19] "is the continuous revision and increase of the heritage of knowledge and thought which comes within its sphere. In the case of law this function is peculiarly important. Law is the framework of the social machine, and if a sufficient number of instructed, free and fertile thinkers could set themselves to ask in the light of our modern knowledge of history, politics and psychology, what are the purposes of law, and by what means those purposes can be attained, an incalculable improvement in human relations might result."

Law is thus in touch with all the political and

[19] *Our Social Heritage*, p. 126.

social sciences.[20] The question is, let us say, whether the hours of labor for women may be regulated by statute. That question came before the Supreme Court in Muller v. Oregon, 208 U. S. 412. The brief submitted by Mr. Justice Brandeis, then at the bar, in support of the validity of the statute, supplied a new technique. It is the sociological method in action. The brief did not concern itself to any considerable extent with decisions or juristic conceptions or abstract arguments. It showed by copious reference to authorities in economic and social science all over the world that unrestricted hours of labor for women had been felt to be an evil, and that almost everywhere statutes had been found necessary that the evil might be curbed. In these and like cases, the problem was at once ethical and social. But the same method is capable of adaptation to problems of a different order. Often the question before the court is concerned with the rule that is to regulate some business enterprise or transaction. The facts of economic

[20] Vinogradoff, *Historical Jurisprudence*, vol. I.

and business life are then relevant considerations. Lord Mansfield heeded them when he built up the law merchant. He did not exhaust their possibilities. The law of bills of lading, of sales, of partnership, of corporations, is still guided, though at times inadequately, by considerations of practical efficiency. The subject has been well considered by Professor Llewellyn of your own law school in a recent address before the Academy of Political Science in the City of New York.[21] "The law," he says, in summing up his conclusions, "needs to act far more quickly than it does in recognizing and giving effect to new business institutions as they arise; it needs to permit to those institutions far greater flexibility than at present in the modification from case to case of their lesser details; it needs to do both of these things with an earnest view to the economic function, and not to the legal incrustations, of the institutions concerned; and the restatement of the law, to satisfy business needs,

[21] X Proceedings Academy of Political Science, pp. 24, 32.

must work, and work vigorously, toward these ends." The Institute is not, however, the only agency that is tending toward the fuller ascertainment of the needs of economic life. The Federal Trade Commission is building up a body of precedent which will fix the proprieties of commercial usage. Comparative law, too, is furnishing example and suggestion, and the points of contact are many between it and jurisprudence.

To the influence of the social sciences, of political economy, of business usage in the development of law, we must add the influence of philosophy. I am speaking now, let it be recalled, not of a philosophy *of* law, not of a theory of the genesis of law, its growth, its end, its function, but of rules and concepts *within* the legal system, and the reaction of general theories of philosophy upon their form and content. The two subjects tend to coalesce. We shall find, for instance, that our theory of the genesis of law has philosophical implications which do not spend their force in determining our notion of the origin of law in general, but spread out and affect our judgment in specific controversies. On the other hand, some problems of philosophy which seem in their general nature to be unrelated to a theory of law, are found, to our surprise, to lie at the root of problems which, at least upon the surface, are purely legalistic. Where shall we find an inquiry more abstract, more divorced, it would seem, from practice, than the metaphysical problem of the nature of truth itself? Who would think offhand that pragmatism had a message for the judge on the bench or the lawyer at the bar? I cannot doubt, however, that the message has been heard. By emphasizing standards of utility, by setting up the adaptation to an end as a test and evidence of verity, pragmatism is profoundly affecting the development of juristic thought. Its truth, if not genuine for the metaphysician, is genuine at least for those whose thought must be translated into action, who are not merely scientists, but craftsmen, and who must ever be satisfied with something less than the perfect and complete ideal.

It teaches each of us to be tolerant of the inevitable compromise. "If by the word 'truth,'" says Santayana, "we designate not the actual order of the facts, nor the exact description of them, but some minor symbol of reconciliation with reality on our own part, bringing comfort, safety and assurance, then truth also will lie in compromise; truth will be partly truth to ourself, partly workable convention and plausibility."[22]

Take again the metaphysical problem of substance and the identity of material things. Law contents herself for the most part with those tests and standards of identity that are accepted by the average mind, untrained in metaphysics. Every now and then, however, she goes farther, though perhaps beyond her depth. A tree grows on a dividing line, its roots in the soil of one owner, and its branches over the soil of another. Dean Pound has shown us the philosophy of Aristotle establishing the identity of the tree and

[22] Santayana, *Soliloquies in England and Later Soliloquies*, p. 83.

adjusting the claims of the contending owners.[23] Grain is sold by a wrongdoer, and after its delivery to an innocent buyer is converted into whiskey.[24] Problems of identity again arise.[25] The whole subject of the confusion of goods is lined with the furrows of Greek philosophers and mediaeval schoolmen. The essential is marked off from the accidental, the constitutive from the derivative, the attribute from the *modi*.[26] There are times, too, when judges have had to struggle with problems of causation.[27] Even more notable has been the influence of theories of metaphysics upon the law of corporations and the theory of juristic persons.

I do not say that the intrusion of philosophy into these fields has been attended always with the happiest results. Some of her exploits may stand as warnings rather than as examples. If

[23] Pound, "Juristic Science and Law," 31 *Harv. L. R.* 1049, 1050.

[24] Silsbury v. McCoon, 3 N. Y. 379.

[25] *Cf.* Buckland, *Roman Law*, pp. 210, 216.

[26] Windelband, *op. cit.*, pp. 52, 66.

[27] Bird v. Ins. Co., 224 N. Y. 47; Lewis v. Acc. Ins. Co., 224 N. Y. 18.

that is so, the undivided blame is not to be put upon the lawyers. A sounder conception of the scope and function of philosophy on the part of the philosophers themselves would have served, in all likelihood, to guide us to a wiser outcome. We should then have concentrated our thought less on abstract conceptions and more on practical results. Professor Dewey tells us that philosophy, once a contemplative study, has suffered a change, and is becoming operative and practical.[28] More and more, he says,[29] it is facing "the great social and moral defects and troubles from which humanity suffers." It is concentrating "its attention upon clearing up the causes and exact nature of these evils and upon developing a clear idea of better social possibilities; in short upon projecting an idea or ideal which instead of expressing the notion of another world, or some far-away unrealizable goal, would be used as a method of understanding and rectifying specific social ills." What is this but to

[28] Dewey, *Reconstruction in Philosophy*, p. 122.
[29] P. 124.

say that the sociological method, which is making itself felt in law, is at work in other fields, and even on those exalted planes which philosophy has reserved as her own peculiar province? If some of the applications of philosophy to law may not incite to emulation, the fault has been, not in supposing that philosophy is a helpful guide, but in the conception of philosophy as alien to experience and life. One must select one's guide with care, even though the candidates for employment are decked in the regalia of the schools. The student does not need to be warned against fertilizing law with the teachings of philosophy. The warning must rather be to be on the watch for the philosophy which, disguised or unavowed, is latent in existing law, to extricate it when it is hidden, to test its truth and value, and to be ready to correct or discard it when it is defective or outworn. The more he knows of philosophy, past and present, the quicker his eyes will be to detect and his judgment to appraise.

There are those who, dismayed by the difficulties of the judicial process when it becomes a creative agency, would keep it to the sphere of imitative reproduction, and leave creation to the statutes. I am not sure but that I should be prepared to join them if statutes had proved adequate in the past to the bearing of such a burden, or gave promise of being adequate within any future now in sight. I have been surprised to see how many partisans the notion of a separation of powers rigid and perpetual—the judges the interpreters, the legislature the creator—is able even in our day to muster at the bar. Some months ago the *New York Law Journal* published letters of its readers, some in praise, some in criticism, of a decision recently announced. The critics, or some of them, went upon the theory that the rule of *stare decisis* was imbedded in the constitution, and that judges, when they departed from it, were usurpers, though the precedent ignored was as mouldy as the grave from which counsel had brought it forth to face the light of a new age. *Stare decisis* is not in the constitution, but I should be half ready to put it there, and to add thereto the requirement of mechanical and literal reproduction, if only it were true that legislation is a sufficient agency of growth. The centuries, if they have proved anything, have proved the need of something more. These tentative and uncertain gropings may be deplored, but they are inevitable, none the less, if we are not to rush blindly into darkness. Unique situations can never have their answers ready made as in the complete letter-writing guides or the manuals of the art of conversation. Justice is not to be taken by storm. She is to be wooed by slow advances. Substitute statute for decision, and you shift the center of authority, but add no quota of inspired wisdom. If legislation is to take the place of the creative action of the courts, a legislative committee must stand back of us at every session, a sort of supercourt itself. No guarantee is given us that a choice thus made will be wiser than our own, yet its form will give it a rigidity that will make retreat or compromise impossible. We shall be exchanging a process of trial and error at the hands of judges who make it the business of their lives for a process of trial and error at the hands of a legislative committee who will give it such spare moments as they can find amid multifarious demands. Even if we could believe that the amateurs would be wiser than the professionals, their remedy would be prescribed too late to help the patient whose disease they had observed. Administered to another, without reckoning a change of symptoms, it might do more harm than good. I do not mean to depreciate unduly the value of the statute as an instrument of reform. Legislation can eradicate a cancer, right some hoary wrong, correct some definitely established evil, which defies the feebler remedies, the distinctions and the fictions, familiar to the judicial process.[80] Legislation, too, can sum up at times and simplify the conclusions reached by courts, and give them new validity. Even then, its relief is provisional and temporary. The cycle is unending. "Code is followed by com-

[80] "A Ministry of Justice," 35 *Harv. L. R.* 113.

mentary, and commentary by revision, and thus the task is never done."[81] The adaptation of rule or principle to changing combinations of events demands the creative action of the judge. You may praise our work or criticize it. You may leave us with the name we have, or tag us with some other label, arbitrators or assessors. The process is here to stay.

Not a little of the suspicion and hostility enveloping the creative activity of the courts in the minds of laymen, if not of lawyers, is due to the prevalent assumption that statute is the typical law, and that the business of the judge is to apply to the facts as found a mandate which to be understood has only to be read. The courts, in the words of Professor Frankfurter, "become the interpreters of self-determining words with fixed content, yielding their meaning to a process of inexorable reasoning."[82] This view of the judicial process would be untenable even if statute did in truth make up the great body of our

[81] 35 *Harv. L. R.*, 113, 117.
[82] Frankfurter, "Mr. Justice Holmes' Constitutional Opinions," 36 *Harv. L. R.* 912.

law. The truth is, however, that it makes up the smaller part. Lord Bryce reminds us in *The American Commonwealth* that the average man in the everyday transactions of life is subject to constraints imposed by the law of the states rather than by the federal government, the law of the nation.[33] That is perhaps not so accurate a statement of ordinary conditions as it was when the *American Commonwealth* was written,[34] but it still approximates to the truth. In like manner, we may say that in the everyday transactions of life the average man is governed, not by statute, but by common law, or at most by statute built upon a substratum of common law, modifying, in details only, the common law foundation.[35] Failure to appreciate this truth has bred distrust of a creative activity which would otherwise have been seen to be appropriate and normal. A rule which in its origin was the creation of the courts themselves, and was

[33] Bryce, *American Commonwealth,* vol. I, chap. 36, pp. 411, 412.

[34] See Pierson, *Our Changing Constitution.*

[35] *Cf.* Pound, *The Spirit of the Common Law,* ch. 1.

supposed in the making to express the *mores* of the day, may be abrogated by courts when the *mores* have so changed that perpetuation of the rule would do violence to the social conscience. No doubt there is need to consider whether men have acted in good faith on the assumption that the rule will be continued. If they have, retrospective change may be forbidden by the same social conscience to which appeal is made for its allowance. Such cases of legitimate reliance upon established wrong—its roots so spreading and so deep that it is to be tolerated, if not respected—are rarer in my judgment than some of us suppose. If abrogation is permissible in cases of extremity, still more plainly permissible at all times is continuing adaptation to varying conditions. This is not usurpation. It is not even innovation. It is the reservation for ourselves of the same power of creation that built up the common law through its exercise by the judges of the past.

This power of creation, if it is to be exercised with vision and understanding, exacts a philosophy of law, a theory of its genesis and growth and aim. Only thus shall we be saved from the empiricism which finds in an opinion, not a prophecy to inspire, but a command to be obeyed. The true point of view has been admirably stated by Mr. Justice Brandeis in his dissenting opinion in State of Washington v. Dawson & Co., 264 U. S. 219, 236. Arguing for the restriction of a rule which had proved itself unworkable, he says: "Such limitations of principles previously announced and such express disapproval of *dicta* are often necessary. It is an unavoidable incident of the search by courts of last resort for the true rule. The process of inclusion and exclusion, so often applied in developing a rule, cannot end with its first enunciation. The rule as announced must be deemed tentative. For the many and varying facts to which it will be applied cannot be foreseen. Modification implies growth. It is the life of the law." Human nature predisposes us to fight against this method, so exhausting in its demands upon strength of mind and body, and to rest on tests mechanical. The delusive hope of certainty satisfies the conscience, only too ready to approve what inertia suggests. Inertia rather than malice was the moving force behind the method practiced by Judge Bridlegoose, the hero of one of Rabelais' satires, who carried mechanical tests to the summit of achievement. Judge Gest of the Orphans' Court of Philadelphia has revived him for us in an interesting address.[86] He decided four thousand cases during his judgeship and all of them by casting lots. Twenty-three hundred and nine of these were appealed, and in every instance on appeal the judgment was affirmed. Here is a fifth method to be added to these already unfolded in our scrutiny of the judicial process. If this be rejected as inadequate, the others will call for an equipment as rich and as varied as the culture of the race. We shall have to be on our guard, none the less, against a state of mind that will lead us to be too distrustful of ourselves. There is danger of a judge's becoming like Pitt's minister who was

[86] Pennsylvania State Bar Association, June 26, 1923.

so irresolute and vacillating that he was constantly late at entertainments because he could not make up his mind in proper time whether to go out or to stay at home.[37] The truth, of course, is that every doubtful decision involves a choice between a nicely balanced alternative, and no matter how long we debate or how carefully we ponder, we shall never arrive at certitude. "In electing a government," says Santayana,[38] "as in selecting a wife, only two or three candidates are commonly available, and the freeman's modest privilege is to declare hopefully which one he wants and then to put up with the one he gets." It is in this spirit of resignation that judges must decide and lawyers must submit.

For the task in truth is one to baffle the wisdom of the wisest. Law is the expression of a principle of order to which men must conform in their conduct and relations as members of society, if friction and waste are to be avoided

[37] John Morley, *Burke*, p. 195.
[38] *Soliloquies in England and Later Soliloquies*, p. 175.

among the units of the aggregate, the atoms of the mass.[39] The expression may be false if those who formulate it, lawyer and judge and legislator, are blind to any phase of the life whose inner harmony they are commissioned to interpret and maintain.[40] No one of us has a vision at once so keen and so broad as to penetrate these unsounded depths and gather in its sweep this enveloping horizon. We can only cling for the most part to the accumulated experience of the past, and to the maxims and principles and rules and standards in which that experience is embodied. Little is the positive contribution that any one of us can hope to make, the impetus that any one of us can give, to the movement forward through the ages. That little will call for the straining of every faculty, the bending of every energy, the appeal to every available resource, within us or without. "Jurisprudence,"

[39] Pound, *Criminal Justice in Cleveland*, pp. 563, 564; *cf.* Gény, *Méthode d'Interprétation en droit privé positif*, vol. II, p. 221.

[40] See Ehrlich, *Grundlegung der Soziologie des Rechts*, p. 384.

says Ulpian, "is the knowledge of things human and divine, the science of the just and the unjust." The definition, famous to the point of triteness though it is, has been scoffed at, not a little, as empty declamation. We have learned to doubt whether the derision was as timely as it seemed. Sir Frederick Pollock has reminded us in a stimulating essay[41] that there may be more of honest truth in the inspiring generality than in many an arid phrase of a colder, if exacter, science. Perhaps our little glimpse into the ultimate, our peep together into the empyrean whence philosophy and law derive their eternal essence, will fill you as it fills me with something of a kindred faith. We shall be spared, at least, the blunder of thinking meanly of our calling. We shall see that our little parish has its vistas that lie open to the infinite. We shall know that the process of judging is a phase of a never ending movement, and that something more is exacted of those who are to play their part in it

41 Pollock, Oxford Lectures, *The Methods of Jurisprudence*, p. 5.

142

than imitative reproduction, the lifeless repetition of a mechanical routine.

I come back in the end to the text with which I started: "Law must be stable, and yet it cannot stand still." The mystery of change and motion still vexes the minds of men as it baffled the Eleatics of old in the beginnings of recorded thought. I make no pretense of having given you the key that will solve the riddle, the larger and deeper principle that will harmonize two precepts which on their face may seem to conflict, and thus to result in an antinomy. I can only warn you that those who heed the one without honoring the other, will be worshiping false gods and leading their followers astray. The victory is not for the partisans of an inflexible logic nor yet for the levelers of all rule and all precedent, but the victory is for those who shall know how to fuse these two tendencies together in adaptation to an end as yet imperfectly discerned. I shall not take it amiss if you complain that I have done little more than state the existence of a problem. It is the best that I can do.

CONCLUSION

We are not yet in agreement about the answer, though in truth it is fundamental and at the basis of our work. We have had courts and recorded judgments for centuries, but for lack of an accepted philosophy of law, we have not yet laid down for our judges the underlying and controlling principles that are to shape the manner of their judging. We do not yet know either our powers or our duties. The tendency that is distinctive good to some is to some distinctive error. What one judge most earnestly believes to be the right method is met by the challenge of men as able and conscientious who say it is the wrong one. I feel very profoundly that at the root of many of our troubles is the need of a better understanding of the existence of this problem, if it is too much to hope just now for a better understanding of the answer. I feel very profoundly that much of the criticism of courts and many of the blunders of courts have their origin in false conceptions, or at any rate in varying conceptions, of the limits of judicial power, the essence of the judicial function, the

CONCLUSION

nature of the judicial process. We may not hope to eliminate impatience of judicial restraint, and even revolutionary encroachments upon the integrity of judicial power, till we settle down to some agreement about the things that are fundamental.

The summons to this better understanding still presses for an answer.